Joan Crawford
Her Life in Letters

MICHELLE VOGEL

FOREWORD BY CASEY LaLONDE

Wasteland Press
Louisville, KY USA
www.wastelandpress.net

Joan Crawford: Her Life in Letters
by Michelle Vogel

First Printing - May 2005
ISBN: 1-933265-46-9

Printed in the U.S.A.

Foreword

Joan Crawford..............Jazz Age flapper, rags to riches shop girl, fashion icon, Academy Award© winning actress and star of over 80 Hollywood movies. Loved by countless millions and reviled by a few others, Joan relied on perseverance and an ability to transform herself over her decades long career.

She began her career as Lucille LeSeur, and then became Joan Crawford beginning with her first film in 1926, *Tramp, Tramp, Tramp.* Joan continued a varied, ever changing five-decade career ending with the 1970 release of the high camp film *Trog.* Although Joan assumed the identities of dozens of characters throughout her career, I simply knew her as "JoJo" for she was my grandmother.

My relationship with my grandmother was brief, but full of vivid memories. I was born in 1972, five years before her death. As my grandmother had relocated from Hollywood to New York City in the late 1950's, she was just a two-hour car ride from my family's home north of Allentown, Pennsylvania.

My mom, Cathy, my father, sister and I would take day trips into the city to see her. The apartment at Imperial House at 150 E. 69th Street is etched in my mind with colorful, Asian inspired decorations. Yes, there were plastic slipcovers on some of the furniture, but I believe she was just psychologically trying to protect her possessions after a lifetime of work.

JoJo would always greet us at the door, usually dressed in a fashionable housecoat. She always wore makeup and one of her amazing wigs. No matter who was at the door, she would look like Joan Crawford, screen legend. When visiting, she treated me to a home cooked lunch in the kitchen, usually some delicious cold roasted chicken. JoJo loved tending to me and my sister, and my parents would sometimes go out for lunch or dinner and have her baby-sit.

She would always have presents for me, not toys necessarily, but more important items that I now consider family heirlooms. One is a child's rocking chair with a needlepoint elephant that she created for the

1

seat. Another is a small bronze turtle from Spain that to this day, sits on my home office desk.

When not visiting, I would try to stay up late to watch *Mildred Pierce* or *What Ever Happened to Baby Jane?* on *The Late Show*. I always took for granted her place as a Hollywood screen legend. For me, she was just JoJo, my grandmother.

Joan Crawford: Her Life In Letters, is a true testament to how my grandmother treated others, not just her friends and peers, but her fans. Her life long dedication to corresponding with the people responsible for making her famous showed how much she cared. The public loved her…and she loved them.

- Casey LaLonde.

A Lady of Letters

"Oh, the thank you notes and best wishes are no big deal. People deserve to be remembered on special occasions, and appreciate being remembered."

- Joan Crawford.

I think it's safe to say we've all been guilty of intercepting a letter that wasn't addressed to us, right? The temptation of a forbidden item, on any level, is exciting, but the reality of possessing a volume of letters from someone as famous, as infamous, as Joan Crawford, is beyond our wildest dreams - until now.

A letter has a certain mystical quality about it. A person's inner most thoughts are written down, sealed within a folded paper vessel and sent off to be read by another person who will either be heartbroken, relieved or elated with the reality of each passing word. But, when that letter is intercepted by someone other than its addressee, *that's* when things get interesting.

This taboo information that's safely sealed for someone else's eyes silently taunts us until we give in and hold it up to the light, squinting as we try to decipher its secret content. If that doesn't satisfy our curiosity, we take the drastic (and somewhat desperate!) step of boiling the kettle in order to carefully steam open the seal. Now that we've officially committed a felon, we can innocently hand the letter over to its intended addressee, fully satisfied......... and with just a hint of guilt...

Sneaky? Yes! But there is something deep within us all that drives us to want to know someone else's business, scrutinize someone else's existence, criticize someone else's life choices. When that "someone" is a movie star, a Hollywood icon like Joan Crawford, our curiosity is immediately piqued to an all time high.

The amount of gossip magazines on the market and the widely criticized aggressive behavior of the paparazzi, to get a story 'at all costs,'

3

only proves that we, the consumer, want to know, need to know, what goes on behind Hollywood's closed doors. Our flood of reality television programs in recent years, and their continued success, only proves our voyeuristic tendencies are now catered to by handing any number of 'reality situations' to us by network television executives. Whatsmore, this invasion of privacy is now considered prime time entertainment.

We watch it on television, we buy it from the newsstands and while it still gets ratings and while it still sells magazines, there will be no boundaries, there will be no privacy, especially for someone who puts themselves into a very public role. The perfect example is the role of an actor. The more protective an actor is of their private life, the more prized the most controversial, embarrassing or informative photo is to the public. If the media can't get the photo or the story needed, the speculation starts, the lies circulate and the rumors spread. This harsh reality may have led to the clever thought process behind Joan Crawford's open lifestyle with the media, and her fans.

For as long as there have been actors, there have been fans. For as long as there have been fans, there's been the media telling them the stories they *want* to hear. That old adage, *"Don't let the truth stand in the way of a good story,"* still rings true today. It was the media's job (especially in Hollywood's heyday) to humanize these people up there on the silver screen, to make the "average Joe" feel that as exciting as it was to sit in darkened room and watch Jimmy Stewart shoot up the bad guys, in reality, he could, if given the opportunity, be a friend. One of the boys.

Hedda Hopper and Louella Parsons were the main two gossip columnists in those golden years of Hollywood. Of course there were many other fan magazines and newspapers that reported the goings on of Hollywood stars but Hedda and Louella were the most trusted, and in the public's eyes, the most believed. However, as trusted as they were by the public, the stars feared them. Get on their wrong side and you were finished! If it was printed in their column, it either happened or it was going to happen, at least the public saw it that way. Yes, they had *that* much power! - With a few choice words, they had enough pull to make or break a career.

Joan Crawford was one of the few Hollywood stars who was capable of being her own publicity machine. She knew who to speak to and she knew if she provided the information herself, there would be no speculative lies printed about her life. With that said, Hedda and Louella were two of Joan's most devoted friends.

Joan knew the public was responsible for the clothes she was wearing, the house she was living in, and for the life she was living. She owed them. So, if the public wanted to know, she'd tell. It was part of her

Lucille Fay LuSueur with her mother, Anna Bell.

job. But, unlike many of her peers, she seemed to revel in it. She was an open book, and the public, *her* public, ate it up.

It was once said, *"Joan Crawford, the star, was not born. She was built."* A big-eyed, uneducated Texas girl named Lucille Le Sueur created her out of glad rags, a set of beautiful bones, a hank of fiery red hair -- and a whole lot of nerve. "Joan Crawford" was an image designed along classic lines. No matter what the current fashions she always looked sleek, fleet, available, and utterly modern. She was built to last.

The power magazines of the day like *Photoplay*, *Screenland* and *Movie Weekly*, were freely invited to her home and given access to photographing her in any room of their choosing. Photographic spreads entitled, "Joan Crawford At Home" or "The Real Joan Crawford" were published often. Her fans saw Joan cooking, playing with her children, lying by the pool, with accompanying articles answering those common questions like - What's her favorite food? - Her favorite hobby? When will her next film be released? All of it done for the benefit of her fans.

There have been many books written about Joan Crawford over the years, with most of them being released after her death, in 1977. The most widely known Hollywood tell all memoir was of course written by Christina Crawford, Joan's eldest adopted daughter.

Mommie Dearest, made the New York Times #1 non-fiction best seller list shortly after its 1978 release, its success prompted the movie of the same name to follow in quick succession.

Within a year of Joan Crawford's death, both book and film, portraying her adoptive mother as a child abusing monster, made Christina Crawford both rich and not only famous, but infamous.

There has been no greater smear campaign of a Hollywood star than of that undertaken by Christina Crawford. She's made a career, a very lucrative career, out of being a victim, and miraculously, her fifteen minutes of fame is showing no sign of ending any time soon. Some 25 years after the books initial release, Christina has just recently released the 25th Anniversary Edition of, *Mommie Dearest*, and with an additional one hundred pages not published in the first edition, it has readers going back for more. Was it all lies? - Was it even the exaggerated truth? Whatever it was, it sold books. It made a great story and at the end of the day, that's what sells.

On March, 19, 2003, I received a brief, one line response to a letter that I had written Christina about this book. It read: *"There is nothing I can add to your work. Best of luck. Christina"* It's the briefest of responses from a woman who once had so much to say, but thinking about it, I guess she's right, what more could she possibly say?

This book is primarily based on Joan Crawford's letters and her compulsive desire to connect with her fans. It is her story, told through the many letters that she'd written to friends and fans throughout her lifetime, and during her fifty-year film career. I will elaborate on the mind boggling volume of letters that she did send out a little later, but for now, let me introduce you to Lucille Fay LeSueur, the little girl who became - Joan Crawford.

*****

A little over a century ago, on March 23, 1904, San Antonio, Texas welcomed a new citizen. At 10PM Lucille Fay LeSueur was born Her year of birth is really the only secret surrounding her life, with it fluctuating between 1904, 1906, even as late as 1908. The latter being the most favored, (obviously because it would make her younger), but cleverly because 1908 was the first year that births were required to be registered. Joan Crawford maintained her birth year to be 1908 throughout her entire life. There was no official way of disputing that information because there were no public records on file prior to that year. Her vain lie, if it was one, was safe for all eternity.

Her biological father deserted the family before she was born and three step fathers came and went by her sixteenth birthday. One of those stepfathers, Henry Cassin, a vaudeville theater manager, renamed his stepdaughter, Billie Cassin, a stage name created for the vaudeville career he had planned for her. The name stuck around, unlike her stepfather, and it was a move to Kansas City that saw Billie and her mother work in a laundry to pay for food, rent and school tuition. The laundry was hot, cramped, and it only ever used wire hangers. No doubt it was this memory that held a lasting affect, spilling over into a phobic aversion to wire hangers as an adult. Unfortunately, it's that infamous "wire hanger" scene that is so often remembered in the cult movie classic, *Mommie Dearest.*

Billie's upbringing was harsh. She was the only working student at St Agnes Academy, Rockingham School and lastly, Stephen's College in Columbia, Missouri. Her daily chores of scrubbing floors, doing laundry, making beds and serving food to her fellow students made her fair game for the class bullies. She was the poor kid, the slave, and she was treated as such. It soon became evident that working for tuition defeated the purpose of being in school. Her chores were so intense she wouldn't finish them in time to make it to class. Eventually she fell behind academically and she withdrew from Stephen's College to pursue her love of dance.

She started working as a sales girl and elevator operator at Harzfeld's department store to pay for professional dance lessons. She entered dance contests whenever she had the chance and it soon paid off. Still in her early teens, she won a Charleston dance contest, her first, in a humble Kansas City Cafe. It was enough encouragement to keep her working toward her ultimate dream of being paid to do the thing she loved most - perform. Chorus work was plentiful and before long her talent allowed Billie to escape Kansas and dance all over the country. She was dancing in Chicago, Detroit, even New York, and she was the happiest she'd ever been.

Her second, and biggest New York Production, *The Passing Show of 1924*, paid Billie $35 per week to appear in the chorus. After being spotted by Harry Rapf, a supervisor at MGM studios, she was asked to do a camera test comprising of a full face and profile shot, along with a series of facial expressions, consisting of sad, mad, questioning, wistful and coy.

A few days prior to the 1924 holiday season, Billie left the musical revue in order to go back to Kansas to be with her family. On Christmas Day of 1924, she received a telegram from MGM Studios. *"You are put under a five year contract starting at seventy-five dollars a week. Leave immediately for Culver City, California. Contact MGM Kansas City office for travel expenses."*

She wasted no time. On New Years Day of 1925, like many young hopefuls, she left for the bright lights of Hollywood. During this same period, around 1923, it has been widely reported that she was married to a James Welton, divorcing him in 1924, after barely a year of marriage. Their union is a little sketchy, some reports even suggesting they weren't married at all, only living together 'as if' married. A moral sin of the times.

After arriving in Hollywood and scoring her first bit part as a showgirl in the 1925 production, *Pretty Ladies*, several other roles of a similar nature soon followed. The studio realized they had a rising star on their hands and a publicity campaign was swiftly arranged to rename their new starlet. Her real name, Lucille LeSueur was thought to sound too much like "sewer" and her stage name, Billie Cassin, wasn't much better.

The studio's dilemma was the perfect excuse for a national publicity campaign. So, with the headline, "Name Her and Win $1,000," a competition in the March 1925 edition of *Movie Weekly* magazine invited the public to pick a name for the new star of MGM. Several photos of the young starlet appeared in the magazine along with a personal statement from her about the competition. *"I'm quite thrilled over this contest which is to find me a new name,"* smiled a pretty Lucille LeSueur across the luncheon table at the Metro-Goldwyn-Mayer Studios.

"People never have been able to pronounce my name or spell it.," she continued, *" and I told Mr. Harry Rapf, when I found out that through this contest the readers of Movie Weekly were to choose a new name for*

me, that I personally will favor, one which is easy to pronounce and spell, and also easy to remember. Of course it must be a pretty name as well."

The rules of the contest were printed exactly as follows:

Here are a few hints to guide you in the selection of a name:

*It must be short or of only moderate length.

*It must be suitable to the individual, who will use it during her entire picture career.

*It must be euphonious, pleasing and yet have strength.

*It must be a name easy to remember and quick to impress.

*It must not infringe upon nor imitate the name or any other artiste.

Following is a description of this young woman:

*She is eighteen years old, was born in Texas of remote French and English ancestry.

*She is five feet, five inches tall, weighs one hundred and twenty-five pounds, has dark brown hair and large blue eyes and a fair complexion.

*She was educated in private schools, including St. Agnes Academy at Kansas City, Mo., and followed this education with a diploma from St. Stephen's college at Columbia, Mo.

*Tiring of the social life of a debutante, she left home to become an actress. You can help her attain her life's ambition by selecting a good name for her, and at the same time the Metro-Goldwyn-Mayer studio will reward you with a large amount of cash.

*There will be eleven winners. From the best eleven names suggested, one will be chosen for this unnamed screen beauty. $500 will be the reward for it, and the sponsors of the other ten names will be given $50 each.

After weeks of wondering and thousands of entries a telegram dated June 26 is sent to Charles A. Green, head of contracts at MGM. It reads: *"Please note that the judges in the Lucille LeSueur contest have decided on the following name for her: Joan Arden."*

July 10 -
Smith's assistant, Howard Strickling, cables MGM from Loew's Inc. on Broadway: *"We are in a jam over selecting Joan Arden as the winning name. While only one quarter [of the] names submitted by Movie Weekly have been checked over, they find Joan Arden duplicated twice...Essential to change name or it will cost about $1,500.00 extra total prizes...Same thing applies to runner-up names Diana Gray, Joan Gray, Ann Morgan, Peggy Shaw. Please stop publication [of Joan Arden] until you receive definite advice. Wire if anything appeared Los Angeles papers and if you have any suggestions this connection."*

Smith replies to the cable the same day: *"Joan Arden's name has repeatedly appeared in print and if any trouble arises it is purely up to Movie Weekly...Essential this be straightened out immediately. Wire us 25 names from which we can make selection. Please rush!"*

August 18 -
Pete Smith advises all studio departments that Lucille LeSueur's new name is Joan Crawford.

September 23 -
Check # 8382 in the amount of five hundred dollars is issued to Mrs. Louise Artisdale, 149 Dartmouth St., Rochester, N.Y. for "First Prize in Joan Crawford name contest."

With the name fiasco settled, 'Joan Crawford' continued to work steadily throughout 1927 and the first half of 1928. However it was one particular 1928 production, *Our Dancing Daughters*, that catapulted her to stardom. It was a bittersweet time for Joan. After agreeing to meet her biological father on the set of *Our Dancing Daughters*, it was the first and last time she ever saw him. There wasn't a man to that day who hadn't let her down in one way or another and a string of future ex husbands and lovers didn't do a thing to change that feeling. She married into Hollywood royalty when in 1929 she became Mrs. Douglas Fairbanks Jr. Her famous in laws were now none other than Douglas Fairbanks Sr. and Mary Pickford.

With a steady paycheck and a new husband, Joan purchased her first home, a white-stucco mansion at 426 North Bristol Avenue in Brentwood for $40,000. It was to be her home for many years, that famous address was boldly printed at the top of her stationery and sent out to thousands of people each year.

Within four years, by 1933, the marriage to Fairbanks Jr. was over and she was soon spotted out and about with yet another actor, Franchot Tone. By 1935 she became his wife, but marriage number two was over within her usual four-year period. By 1939 they too were divorced. The name of the home and every toilet seat in the house was ritualistically changed with each passing husband.

After several failed marriages and more than a couple of miscarriages, Joan, now single again, realized her only chance of becoming a mother was to adopt a baby. She set the wheels in motion; some say through mafia connections, and on June 11th, 1939, a baby girl was born at Hollywood Presbyterian Hospital. Her biological mother was a student, her father, a sailor. Shortly after her birth, the baby girl was taken to Joan's Brentwood Mansion and promptly named, "Joan Jr.".

The laws of California didn't yet allow a single woman to adopt a child, so Joan took the baby to Las Vegas, Nevada, to file the necessary papers there. Once there she officially adopted and renamed her new daughter. From that day on Joan Jr. was known as Christina - Christina Crawford.

In the years to follow, Joan adopted three more children. Christopher, Cathy and Cindy. The two girls were always referred to as "twins." The information on the birth parents of the twins varies depending on whom you speak to, but Cathy and Cindy maintain they are indeed biological sisters.

Cathy's son, Casey, confirms this, "I will not speak on how Joan "acquired" Christina and Christopher, but my mother (Cathy) and (Cindy) were legally adopted in Tennessee. Through research, my mother and Aunt Cindy actually found their birth parents in Tennessee. We first visited the birth family in 1989. They were in fact fraternal twins, and their mother died several days after giving birth. We met their birth father in 1989 and he passed away in the mid-1990's. Christina has made many claims against these facts and she is wrong.

As for Uncle Christopher, I can't even recall the last time I saw him in person. I am thirty two, so I must have been five or so. My most embarrassing experience concerning Christopher was in 1987 (high school), when his family appeared on a talk show, making a public plea to their father to contact them. Christopher had abandoned the family. As for Christopher, from what I understand, he has always had some type of dependency problem. His family mentioned it during their television appearance. I did some research a few years ago, and found a New York Times article stating that authorities had labeled Christopher a "delinquent" after shooting out some street lights on Long Island in 1958.

I had not seen my Aunt Christina since about the same time. My mother (Cathy) refused to have any contact with her following the publication of Mommie Dearest. I do not blame my mother. The book is filled with Christina's lies and mangled childhood perceptions. My mother had such wonderful memories of Joan that she couldn't reconcile Christina's hate.

I do not know precisely what I would do if I encountered Christina. She single handedly ruined my grandmother's reputation. Joan's successful transition from silent to sound movies, many decades of reinventing herself for new audiences, and winning an Oscar for Mildred Pierce were all scuttled for a time because of a child's faulty memories."

By 1942, Joan made Phillip Terry husband number three. Yet another four-year union ending in divorce by early 1946. Joan filed the papers on the grounds of *"cruel and inhuman treatment."* Despite her personal life being in tatters, Joan reached the pinnacle of her career in 1946 with an Oscar nomination for *Mildred Pierce*. On March 7th, the night of the awards, Joan was too sick to attend the ceremony.

It has been widely reported that Joan staged her illness, a convenient excuse to avoid attending the awards and face the possible risk of humiliation and defeat. Shortly after the announcement of her victory was made, reporters swamped her house along with director, Michael Curtiz to deliver the gold statue to the "Best Actress of the year." Joan was interviewed and photographed in bed, with Oscar - the statue. And miraculously, since her win, she felt so much better.

Joan's last marriage to Pepsi Cola boss, Alfred Nu Steele, was on May 10, 1955. No time for divorce here, Alfred died in his sleep on April 19th, 1959, making Joan Crawford a grieving widow for the very first time. Years after his death she bestowed him with an almighty compliment, *"he was the only man I ever truly loved,"* she said. Whether it be divorce or death - It is interesting to note the coincidence of this marriage again lasting the usual run of four years, and coincidentally, this time it was also husband number four!

Joan, the widow, continued to reside in the newly decorated New York Penthouse at 2 East 70th Street, but the couple's lavish spending habits, including the $500,000 renovation of the NY penthouse just three years prior to Alfred Steele's death left their collective finances in ruin. By May, Joan was elected by the Board of Directors of the Pepsi-Cola Company, taking over the role of her husband, until she was forced out in 1972. She still remained a spokeswoman for Pepsi, working for the soda company in one way or another for more than a decade after her husband's death. She successfully juggled her commitments with Pepsi and that of her now ailing film career; it was the busiest she had been in years, yet her finances were still in a mess.

It was the 1962, cult classic, *Whatever Happened to Baby Jane?* that helped boost Joan's bank account and her career (briefly) back to where she desperately needed it to be. The downside? Her co-star was none other than her life long arch enemy.......... Bette Davis!

On screen and off, the public were treated to a Joan Crawford/Bette Davis showdown and they weren't disappointed. With both actresses sharing in the profits of the film's gross, the pay off of working with Bette Davis meant financial stability for Joan. The Crawford/Davis feud was legendary in Hollywood circles. The bitchy public comments expressed about each other were just as dramatic, if not more entertaining, than their acting.

Joan Crawford on Bette Davis:

In 1973, Joan talked about the make up used in *Whatever Happened to Baby Jane?* - *"I am aware of how Miss Davis felt about my make up in "Baby Jane," but my reasons for appearing somewhat glamorous were just as valid as hers, with all those layers of rice powder she wore and that ghastly lipstick. But Miss Davis was always partial to covering up her face in motion pictures. She called it 'Art.' Others might call it camouflage - a cover-up for the absence of any real beauty."*

In an interview after *Whatever Happened to Baby Jane?* was released, Bette referred to Joan and herself as 'we two old broads.' Joan sent Bette a note on her traditional blue imprinted stationery. *"Dear Miss Davis, Please do not continue to refer to me as an old broad. Sincerely, Joan Crawford."*

On the set of *Baby Jane*, Joan was asked about the differences between herself and Bette Davis, Joan said - *"Bette likes to rant and rave. I just sit and knit. She yelled and I knitted a scarf from Hollywood to Malibu."*

Bette Davis on Joan Crawford:

"She was Hollywood's first case of syphilis"

"I wouldn't sit on her toilet"

"That bitch has slept with everyone at MGM, except Lassie, and even then I'm not sure".

"I wouldn't piss on her if she were on fire."

Bette Davis actively avoided Joan Crawford at Hollywood functions. When asked why, Bette said." *You hang around that woman long enough and you'll pick up all kinds of useless shit.*"

Joan insisted that only Pepsi be available on the set of *Whatever Happened to Baby Jane?* - After weeks of drinking Pepsi, Bette screamed, "*Who do you have to fuck around here to get Coca-Cola?!!*"

The verbal insults even spilled over into physical pranks on the set of "Baby Jane" - One scene in the film called for Bette to kick Joan down the stairs. Bette didn't do the "make believe" kick that was pre rehearsed, using the scene to take out her many years of pent up frustrations she gave Joan a good swift kick, with feeling! Joan had plans of her own and got her revenge in another scene where Bette was supposed to drag a lifeless Joan across the floor. Joan tied weights to herself and as a result, Bette strained her back as she struggled to drag the extra weight. This incident and subsequent injury held filming up for several days, until Bette recovered.

Their pranks didn't end on the film set either. Bette Davis got the ultimate revenge when the Academy of Motion Picture Arts and Sciences announced their Academy Award nominations. She received a Best Actress nod for her role in *"Baby Jane,"* whilst Joan was snubbed completely. Joan was furious but quickly went to plan B. She wrote letters to the other four nominees, congratulating them on their nominations and offering to accept their award on their behalf, (should they win) and couldn't make it to the ceremony.

Anne Bancroft won for her role in *The Miracle Worker* and because she couldn't attend Joan gleefully accepted the award on her behalf. Somewhere in the auditorium that night, Bette Davis fumed as she watched Joan Crawford take the stage and accept the award for the actress who beat her out for the Oscar she so desperately wanted. It was to be her last chance of adding another one to her collection.

In *Bette Davis Speaks* by Boze Hadley, Bette Davis spoke publicly for the first time of the apparent 'Crawford sabotage' - *"I was so sure I'd get the Academy Award for 'Jane,' partly to make up for 'All About Eve,' but also for my body of work since the first two. Then, that Crawford bitch sabotaged me, and when Anne Bancroft won, Crawford got on stage to accept Bancroft's award for her! - She'd arranged and schemed, planned everything. She ran a bad mouth campaign against me."*

When Bette Davis passed away, (in 1989) surprisingly, among her possessions was an 8 x 10 black and white photo of Joan Crawford. It was a typical head shot glamour photo of Joan in her heyday, with one exception, her teeth had been blacked out! Despite their vicious, albeit entertaining feud, noted Hollywood columnist, Liz Smith summed both women up in one short sentence," *We will never ever see their likes again.*"

In the years that followed, Joan Crawford made a few forgettable films, worked for Pepsi until 1972 and promptly retired from public life after seeing a 1974 photo of herself that she despised so much, she withdrew into a self imposed public exile.

Joan Crawford's career transcended silents to talkies, she had an impressive eighty plus films to her name over a career span of some fifty years. She was not just an actress, she was a movie star. She made it, she lived her dream, and now, it was time to bow out gracefully.

By April of 1977, Joan's weight dropped to a mere 85 pounds. She refused to see a doctor or even consider leaving her New York apartment to spend her final days in a nursing home, saying, *"I'll be damned if I'll let myself end up in a cold hospital room with a tube up my nose and another up my ass."*

By early May, she realized the end was near, giving away her beloved Shih Tzu, Princess Lotus Blossom, to trusted friends was in itself a sign that she had all but given up. Two days prior to her death, she told her friend and neighbor, Doris Lilly, that she had spent Mother's Day alone. Cindy and Cathy sent flowers and called her on the phone.

Just a couple of days later, on May 10th, 1977, Joan Crawford was dead. Newspapers reported she was 69 years old. It would be unlike Joan to pass without several versions of her death being told. Here are four versions previously published:

According to *Joan Crawford: The Last Word* by Fred Lawrence Guiles - Joan insists on getting out of bed and making breakfast for a dedicated fan that stayed by her bedside all night. She takes some pain pills (for her back) and goes to sleep, never to wake. Her maid finds her mid-morning.

According to *Joan Crawford: A Biography* by Bob Thomas - Joan insists on getting out of bed to make breakfast for her housekeeper and dedicated fan, who both stayed overnight. Joan returns to her bedroom to begin watching her soap operas. She calls out to the two women to make sure they are eating the breakfast she prepared. Then she dies.

According to *Joan Crawford: The Raging Star* by Charles Castle - Having spent the last ten days bedridden, suffering discomfort and incontinence, at 9:30 a.m., Joan asks the full-time nurse assigned to her care to direct Miss Bernice O'Shatz (the dedicated fan) go out on an errand (buying a bedpan) so that she can give the nurse some confidential notes. The nurse goes to the kitchen to make Joan some tea and upon her return, Joan is dead. An embolism has formed in Joan's circulation and blocked the arteries to her heart, resulting in a heart attack.

Lastly, as quoted in *Mommie Dearest* by Christina Crawford – "On the morning of May 10, Joan is attended by one woman. The woman realizes that the end is near and begins to pray, at first silently and then out loud. Joan hears the words, raises her head and declares, 'Damn it...don't you *dare* ask God to help me!' and then dies."

Of course, Christina's account of her mother's death is the most dramatic, which brings me back to *that* book. It has to be said, the catalyst, the final straw, for the very existence of *Mommie Dearest* was the tenth provision in Joan Crawford's Will. It read as follows: "*It is my intention to make no provision herein for my son Christopher or my daughter Christina for reasons which are well known to them.*" The twins, Cathy and Cindy, both received an equal amount of $77,500 each. The bulk of Joan's estate (which had an estimated worth of $1 million) went to various charitable organizations.

Both Christina and Christopher contested the Will and ended up getting a settlement of $55,000 each. By the time legal fees were paid, their cash in hand settlement was closer to $10,000. This menial payout was pocket change compared to the future income that Christina Crawford's book would generate.

Mommie Dearest, the book, was released in the fall of 1978. It's horrific accounts of child abuse by the hand of her adoptive mother, Joan Crawford, saw it enter the New York Times best-seller list at number five and subsequently stay on the list for an amazing forty-two weeks. In May of 1978, Christina signed a contract with Paramount studios for a film based on her memoirs. The film of the same name, *Mommie Dearest*, is now a cult classic. Faye Dunaway played the role of Joan Crawford. It is interesting to note that nine other actresses turned down the part for fear of offending Joan's still powerful Hollywood friends.

It is often said, there is no such thing as bad publicity, but in Joan Crawford's case, the allegations were so bad, that bad publicity stuck. Some twenty years after *Mommie Dearest* was published, people still associate the name Joan Crawford with that of a child-abusing monster, who just happened to be a movie star. Aside from her staunch fans, her prestigious film career has become a secondary memory to the greater majority of the public.

Christina's story is exactly that, "her story." With the publishing of *Mommie Dearest, after* her mother's death, there can be no Joan Crawford defense from beyond the grave. Hardly a fair fight, but Christina accomplished what she set out to do, she managed to get the last word.

Christopher Crawford is a Vietnam veteran and rarely speaks of his upbringing in public. In a rare interview published November 26, 1978 and reprinted in *Parade: Walter Scott's Personality Parade* (1995) - Christopher says, "*I know it's a terrible thing to say but I hated J.C (which is how he refers to Joan Crawford). She was evil and mad, and I don't think she ever cared about me. All she ever cared about was her career.*

She adopted me and the three other kids because it was good publicity, good for image."

Cathy and Cindy, the twins, have commented briefly on the controversy surrounding their mother, Cathy said," *I think Christina was jealous. She wanted to be the one person she couldn't be - mother."* Cathy admits the fact that Joan did indeed discipline them, but there were never any beatings or incidents with those infamous wire coat hangers. *"I think Christina must have been in another household,"* she said. On her feelings for her sister, Christina, Cathy states, *"I just can't feel for anybody who would do that to their own mother. It's very immoral."*

Joan Crawford was a perfectionist. She expected perfection in everything she did and from everyone associated with her. Right or wrong, that included her children. She pushed herself to be the best she could possibly be, rising from the pits of scrubbing laundry floors as a teenager to becoming the leading lady of MGM - A movie star!

Joan Crawford lived the ultimate rags to riches tale and once she made it, she worked damn hard to keep herself on top. Upon her death, Christina worked even harder to unravel that work, to destroy the very image that her mother had so proudly created. How ironic is it that this child, who was said to be adopted for publicity reasons, to help strengthen her public image, was the reason behind her ultimate downfall.

In hindsight, the one positive aspect of this hateful smear campaign was that Joan Crawford didn't live to see it. Had she been alive, the very existence of *Mommie Dearest*, both book and film, surely would have killed her.

Fans, Friends,
and Fizzy Drinks...

"You have to be self reliant and strong in this town. Otherwise you <u>will</u> be destroyed."

- Joan Crawford.

The Crawford fans were a loyal bunch. Almost to the point of worship, they would eagerly eat up every piece of information they could about their queen, Joan Crawford. What better way to connect with them than to release a newsletter, all about herself, with a personal letter written by her, to them, in every issue. It was just another part of the Crawford publicity machine that ensured her fans knew anything and everything, all the time.

In a September 1956 issue, Joan writes, *"Don't you think we have the nicest club newspaper in the whole world? I am always so excited when I see it in the mail, and it's always full of wonderful surprises for me...Martha Kaye's article on the Academy-award presentations was accurate beyond words. I think she has ink in her veins because she is going to make a wonderful reporter."*

Many of these hardcore fans had remained devoted to her since the 1920's, some fifteen hundred of them would write to her on a regular basis. They would learn not only about her upcoming films but also about the personal side of the woman they worshipped. Her favorite color was green and she always slept in white pajamas. Her favorite perfume was Jungle Gardenia, upon knowing her fragrance of choice; bottles of Jungle Gardenia would instantly arrive at her house from admirers everywhere. She wore a size four shoe. She took at least four showers a day, but taking a bath was out of the question. The thought of sitting in her own bath water made her nauseous. She called herself "Elephant Annie" because she never forgot, anything - ever! She never forgot where she came from, and she never forgot the people who put her on the pedestal she so loved to be on. It was all because of her fans.

Co-stars were equally as fascinated with her eagerness to please. Scott Brady, one of Joan's co-stars in the western, *Johnny Guitar*, discovered Joan on a Sunday (her only day off), signing hundreds of fan letters in her hotel room. *"Joan, why don't you hire a secretary to sign your name?"* he said. She replied in true Crawford fashion. *"Why would I do that, after all, there is only one Joan Crawford!"*

Whilst filming *Female On The Beach*, the company continued filming through the Christmas break of 1954, not wrapping until 1.30 pm on December 30th, the day before New Years. As cast and crew gathered for a long awaited holiday drink, they all left the studio to return home to their families, all except Joan. She had work to do, dictating letters into her voice recorder.

When it wasn't her latest film keeping her occupied it was her duties to Pepsi that most certainly did. The soft drink company used her as a promotional tool, running full-page ads with her name and likeness in newspapers everywhere. Their advertising was aimed primarily at Joan Crawford appearing in person at a new bottling plant. Her appearance would turn the once boring factory openings into a media circus. Thousands of people would be in attendance, all of them waiting to see Joan cut a ribbon and declare the plant open.

An astounding crowd of 60,000 people turned out for the Birmingham, Alabama, plant opening. Joan signed autographs steadily for four hours, only downing her pen in defeat after her hand became too tired to hold it. Within two days, 103,000 people toured the new Miami bottling plant and some 30,000 Spanish-speaking residents accepted the plants invitation for a tour on day three.

The crowds were often so thick, a back door, or even a loading dock was used to get Joan to safety. As well as signing photographs, she posed for photographs with fans and local Pepsi executives, always insisting she have a copy for her own files to remind her of the people and names she should remember. Whilst being chauffeured to and from bottling plants and airports, the limousine driver was given strict instructions to travel no faster than forty miles per hour. This gave her enough time between engagements to sign photographs and dictate letters.

Despite having a terrible fear of flying, Joan's demanding Pepsi schedule forced her to overcome that fear as best she could. Eventually she would take the company plane, both nationally and internationally, for appearances all over the world. She would be briefed prior to landing on who would be at the meetings and the bottling plant openings.

A certain time frame was allocated for signing autographs and when it came time to leave, Joan would discreetly trail off the signing by walking to her exit, taking one step further as she signed one more item, smiling and signing she would step through the crowd and into her waiting car. Once inside the vehicle she would dictate more letters and on the flight home she would jot down the names and descriptions of the people she'd met throughout the day. This information would go into her personal file for future reference. If there was a spare moment before landing, she used it, once again, to dictate even more letters!

By 1974, after being officially retired from Pepsi, she became increasingly reclusive. Her most telling sign of her withdrawal from public life was her Christmas letter of the same year. In part, *"With the economy and the world situation as they are, next Christmas and thereafter, the time and energy I spend greeting each of you will be devoted instead to the charities which are so important to the less fortunate people, especially children of the world. This, I believe, is the true meaning of Christmas."*

Her closest friends would still persist and call her often to arrange a dinner out, she'd often accept the invitation, only calling at the last minute to cancel, ironically using her letter writing as an excuse as to why she couldn't make it. Leo Jaffe and his wife made countless lunch and dinner dates with Joan, each one was canceled with the the explanation that she couldn't possibly attend because she was working on her correspondence from five in the morning until eleven at night. It was probably true.

It is without a doubt that the unflattering photographs published of Joan and her lifelong friend, Rosalind Russell, was the main reason behind her reclusive behavior. At the time, Rosalind Russell was an elderly woman too. The drugs she was taking to treat her painful arthritis had bloated her badly and like Joan, her age and illness had simply caught up. The photo didn't lie. Joan Crawford was well aware of the truth of a camera and after seeing that photo, she was damned if she'd ever be photographed in public again.

As promised, by 1976 the Christmas greetings had become fewer, and the ones that she did write, she stated that from now on she'd be devoting her energies to charity. Her closest of friends were sent a more personal note, along with a photo of herself and Princess, her beloved Shih Tzu. Once again the photo told the story. There was pain in her eyes, yet in that true Crawford fashion, she smiled for the camera and didn't once utter a word of complaint.

Her friends would call her on the telephone and hear a cheerful voice greet them warmly. Never would she use that time to complain to them about the pain that was her now constant companion. They would still persist and ask her out on lunch and dinner dates, only to receive the excuse that she's quite happy to stay at home with Princess and watch her favorite soap operas on television.

Adding to her already mountainous volume of correspondence, she would write down the names of any new actors that she would see on TV and send them a note of praise. A flood of letters, cards and flowers boosted her morale on her birthday in 1977, but it was momentary. Her health was rapidly declining, as was her weight (she was now 85lbs), she was in constant pain. Any medical treatment was flatly refused, the only painkiller she'd allow in her apartment was aspirin, a drug strong enough to alleviate the common headache, but certainly not cancer of the liver or pancreas, which her symptoms suggested she had. The only concession she allowed herself was a hospital bed in her room. The various positions operated by a remote control, alleviated the pain in her back and allowed her to watch TV more comfortably. She now had a secretary answer her phone, responding in her own time to the messages she felt were the most important.

Her two constant daily companions were here housekeeper and a lifelong fan who tended to her every need. On her good days she would get out of bed and sit at her desk, attending to her letters until her pain became too much. Not giving up entirely she would return to bed and sign her letters on a bed table that she rested on her lap. Her letters were now her only form of communication with the outside world, they were fewer now, but still, she continued to write as many as she could, daily. Some of her last correspondence was to her closest Hollywood friends. Sally Blane's husband, Norman Foster, had passed away in 1976 and Joan sent her friend a handwritten letter of condolence and reminiscence reflecting on the loss of her own husband, now eighteen years before. *"Dwell only on the joys,"* she said.

Virginia Grey, another Hollywood friend, received a letter from Joan about her adjustment to moving to a smaller apartment. The sprawling Brentwood mansion was now only a memory for her, as was the luxurious New York apartment she once shared with her late husband, Al Steele. Joan wrote that she was 'content beyond belief,' but having spent a solid year on only finding places for her most loved things, she gave the advice her lawyer's wife had given her. *"Never love anything that can't love you back."*

Ironically, it was a line that Joan had lived by her entire life, especially when it came to her fans. They loved her and she loved them back. It was those fans who gave her some of the most fulfilling and consistently loyal relationships of her life.

Receiving the mail was her favorite part of the day, a letter from someone special giving her more joy than anything money could buy. She would beam with excitement as she looked over her daily mail. Amongst the masses of fan letters were letters and notes from her equally famous contemporaries. She was particularly excited the day she received a letter from Barbara Stanwyck and Katharine Hepburn, on the same day. Not that these letters were considered any more important to her than her fan letters, she just wanted to be remembered, by her friends, by her fans, by everyone.

As an old woman, and in her last Christmas greeting before her death, Joan Crawford wrote a humorous, albeit sarcastic, 1976 Christmas card to persons unknown. She said, *"I am so at peace with the world that I'm even having good thoughts about Bette Davis."* It seems that time, age or maybe even selective memory can wash away the jealousy and bitterness of years gone by.

Letters From Joan

"Look, there's nothing wrong with my tits, but I don't go around throwing them in people's faces!"

- Joan Crawford on Marilyn Monroe.

There have been a multitude of biography type books written on Joan Crawford over the years, but none have been solely dedicated to the art of her compulsive letter writing. During the 1960's and 70's, as her career was winding down, it was not unusual for her to mail out a staggering five thousand letters a month! During the holiday season, between Thanksgiving and the New Year, (a mere six week period) she would personally type, sign and mail ten thousand letters!

If someone took the time to write her, the least she thought she could do was respond. Whenever she received a thank you note, the sender would receive a thank you note for their thank you note! She *always* had the last word. During her reign at MGM she would write letters between takes in her dressing room. She would sign photos in the car on the way to the studio in the morning, and again on the way home from the studio that evening. The weekends were also used to catch up with her correspondence and write or type letters.

An almost pen pal type relationship developed between herself and many of her most devoted fans. During her retirement, from 1974, through to her death in 1977, she did nothing but correspond with friends, fans, Pepsi dealers, fellow actors, anyone and everyone. Her closest friends would receive letters written entirely in long hand, others would get typed notes signed "Joan Crawford," "Joan" or "J.C.," depending on the closeness of their relationship. Her pale blue stationery with the simple heading of "Joan Crawford" averaged an annual mail out of 70,000 - During her fifty-year career, it is estimated that she sent over three million letters!

She answered every single piece of fan mail herself, with one exception. She ignored all correspondence from her former classmates at Stephens College. The same students who bullied her for being poor, now wrote to her with a "remember me?" attitude. Joan remembered only too well and she took great satisfaction in ripping up their letters before moving onto opening the next letter, (one that she would reply to with pleasure), as long as it wasn't from a former classmate!

Hollywood today is a world away from 'old Hollywood.' Back in Hollywood's heyday, fans were treated with respect. The stars knew only too well that these people, the film going public, were the reason they were sitting in their luxurious mansions and wearing their designer clothes. The fans paid for that lifestyle, upset them and you're history.

So, was this obsessive correspondence really just another part of the Joan Crawford publicity machine? If it was, she did it well. Her letters always showed genuine concern, warmth, appreciation and love to the person she was writing to, even to the extent of knowing and remembering their spouses names, their children's names, their career concerns, details that some close family members would so commonly forget.

There's no doubt that Joan Crawford made hundreds, even thousands of lonely people very happy with her constant correspondence. In hindsight, maybe she was the lonely one? Constantly needing that reassurance of love from her fans to feel worthy. Whatever the reason, for the average person, this much letter writing would be an arduous full time job in itself - But, Joan Crawford was not the average person. For Joan Crawford this was just a necessary sideline that went with the responsibility of being a movie star. The following collection of letters pieced together in chronological order, shows yet another facet to Joan Crawford, the person. Her thoughts, her words, her letters - The last word.

The Letters...The Early Years

"She was forever sending thank-you cards, and had fancy stationery with 'JC' on it.... Christ! - She did that to everyone, even reporters. With that woman you could 'nevah' be sure what her motives were, and I sent her presents back! "

- Bette Davis.

In 1923, the earliest letter to date, a young, Billie Cassin writes besotted love notes to her boyfriend, Nig Stafford. Because of the varying thoughts on her year of birth, it's estimated that Joan would be between the ages of seventeen and nineteen when these love letters were written. She was still attending Stephens College, in Columbia, Missouri, at the time.

These letters show an insecure, sensitive young woman, who ironically went on to become one of the toughest, most determined women in Hollywood history. This is Billie Cassin, *before* she was Joan Crawford, in oh so many ways...

Stephens College, Columbia, Missouri - 1923 - Handwritten letter - To "Mr. Nig Stafford," (an early boyfriend) ~

My Darling, Nig -
You see, I am true to my promise, I finally reached my room in safety, anyone sure could find me tho, cause there's mud from first floor to my room on third! I think I had two or three inches of mud on my feet. Well, anyway I sure had a great time and enjoyed your company immensely. Think of the risk I took. But believe me it was surely worth it, and I would do it again, just to be with you dear. I'm terribly sorry that Johnny didn't like his date, perhaps next time I can get my pal for him, she sure is a fine sport. I know you are terribly busy dearest, but spare a few minutes and answer this brief note. And may I expect an answer tomorrow? - Good night dear heart -

- Lots of love, Your Billie.

A publicity photo of Joan from Tide of Empire (1928). It reads, "Dan – Josephita (her character name) she is very sad, could you make her happy by writing to Joan." Incidentally, this film was abandoned and remade in 1929 with Renee Adoree in the main role of Josephita.

A playful pose.

Joan hasn't exactly been portrayed as the chaste good girl over the years; however, the following letter shows another side to her. There's a refreshing innocence to this letter, together with a desperation and realization that her behavior may have ended her cherished relationship.

It seems Nig, Joan's boyfriend, isn't happy with her "lack of affections." Here she answers his frustrated letter with an equal amount of frustration, telling him that in her opinion, "true love isn't all physical!"

Stephens College - Columbia, Missouri - Handwritten, twelve-page love letter to an early boyfriend, Nig Stafford, signed Billie as in "Billie Cassin."

My Nig dearest,

I realize that I was in a bad humor when I wrote that last letter and regretted sending it since I mailed it this morning. You said you thought of me in an entirely different light. How is that dear? Really it's hard for me to begin this after what has taken place, but I had no idea you cared so much until I read this last dear letter, which I received tonight. Oh Nig, love, if I have disappointed you in any way I am not fit to love and really am so sorry I've treated you like I have. But I have been so neglectful that I dare not ask or hope for your forgiveness. I ask only that you try and find it in your heart to believe at least part of what I am going to say, every word of which I swear is the truth.

Nig, I have not been my real self. Why? I do not know and don't suppose anyone here does either. I realize that I have not dated personally like I portrayed myself initially. Really, I don't see how I stand being away from your dearest when I love you, oh so very much. I shall show some of my affection, I know but as I said before I have not been myself. Generally, I am of a very affectionate nature and show it considerably, but I've been told when one shows me affection too much, the other gets tired and so I tried not to show it too much, there has been times when I wanted to oh so badly just tell you personally how much I really loved you but something seemed to hold me back so I didn't, what it was, I can't say, but it did just the same.

Nig, please, please I beg of you not to mention petting parties to me again when I've given up all that bunk just for you and then you throw it up to me, Darling sweet heart, don't you say I don't know true innocent love when I have it. I do Nig, I feel it, I see it, oh I do know my love for you is true innocent love.

What do you mean by "I should thrill you in a different way, a wonderful way" - I must be awfully dumb but I do not understand. I fully realize that there is nothing to be ashamed of by our love, Nig, perhaps this little misunderstanding will bring me to my senses and make me be

28

A 1928 portrait shot.

Joan in a close up portrait from *Rain* (1932).

my real true self in the picture but I don't know why I have ailed in such a manner dear.

Yes dearest darling you are worthy of my love that I keep professing to you Yes, "More than worthy." If ever we are lucky enough to be together again, I'm sure I'll do all I can to show you just how glad I was to see you instead of keeping it to myself.

No, I'm not afraid as you seem to think not at all dear. Never do I fear anything when I am with "you!" Honestly, I believe you when you say you really love me. It is such a wonderful thought, loved one. Promise, I do know a true love when I have it.

Another thing is I don't pretend to be clever or charming so therefore I didn't expect it to substitute. So don't judge me too initially at first, give me a fair chance to prove it. Also, I realize that love is not entirely a physical affection so naturally it is mostly mental. I'm young, that I realize, but I also realize that it is not merely fascination but it is truly "true love."

Perhaps you do not know it when you have it, you have it and just do not realize it, so there you are. What shall we do? I know the one and only. To begin all over and to our real true selves and show our affections to one and other and show our true love - Darling, what do you say to my suggestions?

My sweetheart, please forgive everything I've done and love me - And I'll do all I can to live up to your expectations and you to mine and write me later when you're home and lots when you go and lots when you come back. I know not where you keep my picture but I would gladly give a year of my life to be in its place right now. Will you write about twice as much as you wrote me so I'll ring off and impatiently await an answer. So sweet of you to send it so I got it tonight.

- All my love, always for you from your everlasting loving, Billie.

Undated - Going by the clues within the body of the following letter, Joan mentions her impending 21st birthday, so it has to be the month of March in the year 1925 or 1927. Again, the mystery surrounding her birth year prevents us from making an accurate assessment of the exact year, however, Joan's granddaughter, Carla, confirms Joan's year of birth was definitely 1908.

Joan also poses an interesting question about her future career as an actress. Still uncertain of herself, she asks if he (Dan Mahoney, the addressee) thinks if she'll ever be able to *"keep an audience in their seats, like 'The Three Musketeers' do!"*

Her new film, *The Dancing Girl*, was later released as *Our Dancing Daughters*. This historical fact also gives us a more specific clue

One of the many glamour shots take of Joan Crawford. She was the most sought after Hollywood actress to be photographed because of her near perfect facial bone structure.

as to when the letter was written. *Our Dancing Daughters,* was released in 1928, so that dates the letter a little before the films release, but still of that same year. So, based on scattered clues throughout, it seems Joan wrote this letter in March of 1928. However, her so-called 'clues' go on to create another mystery! With Joan mentioning that she's just about to turn twenty-one, this gives her yet another birth year, this time - 1907!

This is a rare handwritten letter on onionskin paper with an original poem written by Joan, entitled. "A Prayer."

Wonderful Person,

How on earth can you, and do you, write such gorgeously beautiful things in your letters? - Anyone who possesses such beauty of soul well - gee I don't know. You see, I think I'm such a silly fool, because of the simple little things I find beauty in, but when I see you too do the same, oh I just think of how beautiful your soul and heart both are, and still keep on saying. I'm a silly fool, perhaps it's because I can never express myself like you. I try to put into words what I see, and think, and I'm so full inside that I can't. Then comes a letter from you and oh, well, life's such a damn puzzle anyhow.

Anyhow, yes, anyhow, try to make it more so. I'm having a birthday this week, the 23rd and I'll be able to vote. After this one I'm not going to have anymore, so if you ever ask me my age - Remember, this is my last for the next, oh, I don't know for how long. But still, I'll be 21 from this March on. How's that?

Perhaps, Dan someday, I may do something equally as beautiful as the Three Musketeers, make an audience sit in their seats, spell bound, want more, love me, and all that. Do you think I could do all that? I hope you will be proud of me in my new picture, "The Dancing Girl" - I love it, better than anything I've ever done. Maybe you will too, huh? Don't be so cruel. Please write more often. Dan, see if you like this, I wrote it some time ago -

A Prayer
Hail Mary Mother so full of grace
With your lovely Madonna face
You've listened to hundreds of thousands pray
You in your Heaven so fair and so brave
You've heard the sweet prayer of a child
Ever so meek - Ever so mild
The prayer of a mother, you'll hear and understand
Knowing in your heart all mothers are good
A murderer when all hope is gone
Turns to you and threw darkness and dawn

Even the strongest of all mankind
Beg your forgiveness and worship your shrine
But blessed Virgin Mary in your kingdom above
What equals the beauty of a maiden in love?
I know for as a child I prayed to you
And as a mother I prayed for comfort too
But this prayer is neither of child or mother
It's the prayer of a girl who has a lover.

- Joan.

In 1926, Joan, now a young starlet, writes to a fan apologizing for her newly released film, *The Boob*. The original stamped envelope is postmarked, Los Angeles, California, June 14, 1926 and addressed to a Mr. Daniel Mahoney, 2452 Sunset Ave, Dayton, Ohio. A post office correction indicates it was forwarded to him at 2715 Webb Ave, Bronx, New York. It reads as follows:

Saturday Eve - 1926

I just found out a film I made over a year ago called, 'I'll Tell The World,' has been released under, 'The Boob.' I'm so sorry I made such a dreadful mistake. Will you forgive me?
You don't need to tell me it was a terrible picture. How well I know. I wouldn't even go to see the preview.
I'm so glad you enjoyed 'Paris.' I tried so hard to make it a good picture and when people are as lovely as you are to write such lovely letters and congratulate me on my work, I'm terribly happy. It is so sweet of you to compare me with a lovely flower and speak of my work as you do. I only hope you shall always think as you do now. Especially after meeting me, if we ever do.
Thanking you very sincerely from the bottom of my heart, for the interest you have shown. Shall send you a photograph very soon.

The release date of, *The Boob,* was June 17, 1926. Joan's apologies for making a bad film were echoed by the harsh comments in *The Baltimore Sun.* "*A piece of junk. ...The company has simply covered itself with water and become soaking wet, for this tale of a half-dumb boy who turned prohibition agent to convince his girl he had nerve is as wishy-washy as any pail dishwater.*"

In another letter to long time fan, Dan Mahoney, approximately a year or two later, she openly discusses her newfound freedom after the break up with her boyfriend. In an almost desperate plea, she asks him to write to her daily, if he can -

A classic Joan Crawford pose.

A candid shot of Joan on the set of *Forsaking All Others* (1934)

A 30 year old Joan on the set of *Chained* (1934).

Circa 1927 - 1928

Dear Dan,
 How sweet you are to always send me those clippings and what a thrill those last ones gave me. Weren't they grand? Especially the Sun. Oh, what a break they gave me. No doubt you have read or heard about me doing, "Rose Marie" - Yes?
 Oh, so many lovely telegrams and letters have been flowing in, and Dan dear, oh, I'm so happy about it. You know too, I've broken everything off with Michael over two weeks ago. I'm free, white and - twenty-one. 'Thank God!' - Ah Dan, I do need your letters so much, won't you write me as often as you can. I wish it were as often as everyday, if possible. Am doing a quick one before 'Rose Marie' so am working day and night. That lovely thing about 'Faith' ah will you ever, ever realize how it helps to know someone has faith in you? Won't you write some more for my book of original poems?
             - God Bless You, Joan.

 The review of *Rose Marie* in the *New York Times* of February 13, 1928, briefly mentions Crawford as, *"most prepossessing as 'Rose Marie,' but she seems like a girl who flings her part quickly behind her, especially when James Murray holds her in his arms."*

May, 1928 - Handwritten, most likely sent to Dan Mahoney.

Dearest -
 Am rather depressed today. I just came home from the doctor and he made up my mind for me to go to the hospital the day the picture is completed. In a way I'm glad, so as to get the darn thing over with, and too I'm scared to death. God! - The thought of it drives me crazy.
 Am so afraid to see the reviews for 'Across to Singapore.' Bless you for the lovely wire. It's hot as blazes here every day. What a gorgeous tan I could get if I wasn't working. However last Sunday and Monday Dodo (Douglas Fairbanks Jr.) and I went up to Doug and Mary's house and played around in the sun and swimming pool both days. The result was I was one complete freckle. Oh but it's swell. Be a sweet darling person. I'll write again before I go under ether. Pray for me in the meantime.
            - Good night dear. Love, Joan.

 It was around this time; during the filming of *Across To Singapore (1928)* that Douglas Fairbanks Jr. accompanied Joan on a location shot at

Yosemite National Park. As he listened to her sing the *Indian Love Call*, he fell in love. That December, he proposed and she accepted. They were divorced after four years of marriage.

Four page handwritten letter, circa 1928, on Metro Goldwyn Mayer Stationary. To Dan Mahoney of New York. Joan starred alongside John Gilbert in *Four Walls*, the film she mentions seeing a preview of in the below letter. She did not however star in his next film *Thirst*. Mary Nolan replaced her. The film was renamed *Desert Nights*.

Dan -

Some things are awfully hard to destroy aren't they???

I'm afraid dear you've misunderstood me or something. You knew I went back to work, therefore you thought I should write. You did not know this, that I went to work three days after my operation and had to practically be carried, did you? You thought I went to work two weeks later, didn't you? Well, my one-day at work too soon put me back exactly three weeks. I was so weak. I couldn't think of telegrams, letters or anything. In fact, I was quite unable to write, even to my mother. And too, you were the first person I did wire or even send any sort of a message to. My mother didn't hear from me till a week after you did. Don't you see Dan; there are two sides to every story.

Yes, I did tear your letter up, because I know you did not quite understand the situation, for if you did you wouldn't have written it. I have more faith in you than you give credit for. You see, everything happens for the best, perhaps this shall make you fully realize how much faith I have in you (for you've said several times you wish I did have). Please (I ask you now) have faith in me in what is very dear to me "my friendship for you!"

Had a preview of 'Four Walls' and it's said that it is one of the best M-G-M have turned out. And too, 'Dancing Daughters' is being held for a special fall preview. So I have two good ones to my credit now. I'm doing Jack's (John Gilbert) next picture too, called 'Thirst,' a desert story. I start in about two weeks. I'll have to go on location, don't know where yet, but will let you know.

I'm getting all the red off my hair. I had it all put back to its natural color yesterday. It was almost blonde in the last two pictures. Studios raised Cain cause they wanted it to photograph blonde but I said "Nuts" and had it fixed a la naturel. It scared the hell out of me when I looked in the mirror, my hair is real dark brown and I hadn't seen the natural color for so long, it rather hit me in the face. I do like it now that I'm getting used to it. Am scared to death to go to the studio.

How do you like this book I'm writing you? Am still so nervous. I can hardly hold a pen in my hand. However, I tried to write this so you can read it. Do write me and say all is forgiven, won't you please?

- Love always, Joan.

1928 was a big year for Joan, having made a staggering nine films in that year alone, *Our Dancing Daughters*, was the one that officially made her a star. MGM were all of a sudden inundated with mail addressed to 'Joan Crawford.' Because of her popularity her salary was doubled. Joan Crawford had served her time as an uncredited bit player, her name would appear above the title from now on and it would stay there for another four decades.

Overwhelmed with her newfound stardom, Joan drove around the neighborhood at night, taking pictures of her name on theater marquees with her modest box camera. She'd finally made it and she was determined to capture her "so-called" fifteen minutes of fame. Ironically, Joan's fifteen minutes of fame stretched to 50 years!

November 22, 1928 - A profusely apologetic, handwritten letter on Metro-Goldwyn Mayer Stationery - To "Dan Mahoney" with additional post script and co-signed by Joan's then fiancée, Douglas Fairbanks Jr. *Note: "Dodo" is Joan's nickname for Doug Jr.; "Uncle Doug" is her nickname for future father in-law, Douglas Fairbanks, Sr.

Dear Tired Dan -

You see, I did have cause for worry when you were ill and you begged me not to. And I count you as my bestest, truest most devout friend, Dan, and I have been so neglectful lately (or so it seems). No wonder you give up hope of ever hearing from me.

My family just arrived out here, two one week and Mother two weeks later, that's been quite a burden also. Getting a place for them to live. Getting my brother and his wife jobs, and thousands of exhibitors out here having lunch, reporters from the four corners of the earth interviewing you, Mother's Birthday this week, Thanksgiving next, starting Christmas shopping, more law suits, signing new contracts, still getting my house furnished. And worst of all, talking pictures!

On my Sundays off, I sew all day at Pickfair, until Dodo, Uncle Doug, and Mary go mad when they see a needle and spool of thread. Poor blessed Dodo hasn't had much attention lately but as long as he knows I love him, I hope he understands.

Do keep me more closely informed as to your health, dear, won't you? - May I hear from you soon - Please??????

- As ever, Joan

An early portrait of Joan signed, "To Estelle, A perfect darling. May we always be the best of friends. Love from, Joan."

One of the many MGM publicity stills.

One of the thousands of letters sent to Joan Crawford at the MGM mailroom, this one with an uncanny hand drawn portrait of their favorite star. No name needed, just "that face, those eyes," and Hollywood, California.

PS: Dan, Joan's friends are dear to her, she speaks of you incessantly and if you don't mind will you be my friend and allow me the honor and pleasure of yours being yours? - In anticipation, "Doug" Fairbanks Jr.

From the tone of the above letter, it sounds like Dan's nose was a little out of joint at the recent engagement announcement of Joan to Doug Fairbanks Jr. A frequent correspondence developed between Dan and Joan during her early Hollywood years, but with Doug writing his "can we be friends?" post script, he was no doubt trying to calm the waters between old friends, smoothing the way for continued correspondence...for Joan's sake.

April 15, 1930.

My dear Marjorie,
My, how surprised and pleased I am to learn that you have saved five hundred pictures of me: That makes me feel very proud. Yes, I still have my two dogs and am just as fond of them as I have stated in interviews.
My next picture is 'Our Blushing Brides' and Robert Montgomery is playing opposite me. The plot is based on modern situations, along the same lines as 'Our Dancing Daughters,' I hope you will like it.
- Sincerely, Joan Crawford.

It was on the set of *Our Dancing Daughters* that Joan started to receive an increased amount of fan mail. Immediately after the films release, she was flooded with letters. She was so overwhelmed with this public response she not only answered each letter personally, she even licked the stamp and went as far as taking them all to the post office herself! The success of *Our Dancing Daughters* saw MGM double her salary and feature her name *above* the title of her films, as well as on posters and marquees displayed throughout the country.

It is also at this time that MGM paid out over half a million dollars to buy up all copies of a 'sex tape' that was being circulated around town. The silent one reeler said to be entitled, *The Casting Couch*, supposedly showed a nude Joan in some compromising positions that simply weren't good publicity for the 'wholesome' movie star that MGM had since created.

After thinking they'd accomplished what they set out to do, an anonymous man phoned the studio claiming he had several nude shots of Joan that he *would* circulate and wouldn't part with for any amount of money. Not the brightest of blackmail attempts to make since three weeks after this phone call his house was burned to the ground. Both he and the controversial photos perished in the blaze. Coincidence?

May 6th, 1930 - On "JC" initialed letterhead.

Dear Rena,
    Thank you very much for your letter. My hobby is collecting dolls, and my favorite sports are tennis, swimming and golf. 'Our Blushing Brides' is another "Modern." Robert Montgomery is my leading man. I hope you will like it.
        - Best wishes, Sincerely, Joan Crawford.

    Released on August 2nd, 1930, *Our Blushing Brides* was considered a box office bomb. The following review by Lucius Beebe of the *New York Times* praised Joan's performance, yet the film as a whole did little to advance her career. He wrote: *"It is all quite lamentable and would be downright depressing in its spurious elegance if it were not for the humorous and intelligent acting of Joan Crawford, who plats the part of a mannequin with enough assurance for a marchessa and enough virtue for a regiment.*

June 16th, 1930 - A handwritten letter on 'JC' letterhead -

Dear Dan -
    I heard thru a friend of mine that you are leaving for New York soon. I gathered from your letter you were improving, but not to the extent of going to New York. It seems rather odd, Dan, that you should go to New York instead of staying out here in this climate where it is good for you, and which, obviously, New York is not! - It's none of my business I assure you and I don't wish to appear to make it such but merely a suggestion.
    I do think however that I should be the first to know when you were leaving and if it were not too much trouble would you let me know. Do hope you continue improving.
        - As ever, Joan.

January 11, 1932 - To "Genie Chester" in New York City - Hand written letter on "JCF" (Joan Crawford Fairbanks) stationary -

Genie dear -
    Please forgive my seeming rudeness but I've been working dreadfully hard. Even Christmas and New Years Eve. Your gifts to us were too lovely. Douglas loves and adores his book, it is the prize of his

collection and he has not ceased to make everyone who enters the house look at it from corner to corner.

My mules are too grand to wear; as a matter of fact they are put carefully away with a drawer full of new "nighties" Dodo gave me for Christmas, only to be worn on our honeymoon this spring.

I know you must look beautiful with your hair bobbed, not that you looked otherwise with it long. It is more comfortable tho, isn't it? - I'm letting mine grow just shoulder length, as I think it softens my face. Perhaps we will all be in Europe at the same time, who knows? We really don't know the exact date when we can get away from work. I hope we can all be together any way. Again, let me thank you for your lovely things - Do write soon again -

- As ever, with love - Joan.

The "Honeymoon" she speaks of in the above letter is her "second honeymoon" with Douglas Fairbanks Jr.

July 23, 1932 - To "Genie Chester" of New York City - Handwritten letter -

Dear, dear Genie -

How heavenly to look at your gift all in blue and silver. To be very honest I have not cut the ribbon as yet, it is so divine, it seems a pity to destroy it by opening it. Alright, I will anyway ---

We shall soon see for ourselves if London is a man's town and Paris is a woman's. Genie, my sweet, have you any idea how grateful I am to you and how much I love you?

- As ever, Joan.

The above letter is written shortly before Joan and Doug Jr. sail for Europe on a second honeymoon, entirely funded by Louis B. Mayer. During the London leg of their vacation, Joan was so unhappy, so homesick, they returned to the United States ahead of schedule.

September 9, 1933 - To "Genie Chester," a handwritten letter on "JCF" (Joan Crawford Fairbanks) letterhead paper.

Genie dear -

So glad you are having such a restful summer - At present I am holding up production with a sprained ankle - It is the same one I've broken three times and it's painful as the very devil. Write when you feel like it darling. My love to you and your family

- As ever, Joan.

46

It's interesting to note that Joan was still using her "Joan Crawford Fairbanks" stationary in September of 1933, since she filed for divorce on May 13, 1933. In true Joan fashion, shortly after hiring a lawyer to dissolve her marriage, she hired good friend, William Haines to change the toilet seats and redecorate her entire Brentwood estate. She obviously hadn't gotten around to changing her stationary yet.

The film she is holding up production on is, *Dancing Lady*. This movie seemed cursed with both injury and illness. Of course, Joan had her fair share of pain with her sprained ankle and Clark Gable had an emergency appendectomy and held up the beginning of production before cameras rolled. Aside from the two main stars having health problems, the original male lead vocalist slipped a disc and was replaced by Nelson Eddy after jumping awkwardly onto a podium in the "Rhythm of the Day" sequence.

May 17, 1934 - To "Genie Chester" of New York City - On "Joan Crawford" imprinted stationary -

Genie dear -

Your wire was so encouraging - Golly, I was scared, I was shaking like a leaf in a winter wind. I'm so glad you liked the broadcast. How wonderful that you are going to London - How long will you be over there?

I start work again this coming Monday, so it looks like I won't get a vacation till July or August. Do try and see 'Sadie McKee' before it closes and let me know what you think of it. I was pretty unhappy with the way it was cut, perhaps it will make sense - but I doubt it.

Genie, my house is going to be so beautiful, you will not recognize it. Do let me know your plans and when you see Douglas, give him my love. My best to your mother, father and everyone.

- And a very large share of my love for you - Joan.

October 11th, 1934 - On Metro Goldwyn Mayer Studio Stationery to a Mr. Billy Griffiths c/o The Jean Harlow Fan Club in Calcutta, India.

Dear Mr. Griffiths:

Thank you so much for inviting me to join your fan club. I am indeed highly honored. Under separate cover I am mailing the pictures you requested. Wishing you and your club every success.

- I am - Gratefully, Joan Crawford.

An undated handwritten letter on "Joan Crawford" imprinted stationary - However, Joan mentions the recipient of the letter, "Betty,"

47

seeing her new film, *Chained*. Since this particular film was released in September of 1934, the content of the letter helps to date it around the latter part of 1934.

Betty dear -
 You must not let people disturb you. Do what your heart tells you to do - and as long as it does not harm anyone - you will be happy. You write me as you like - if it's four times a day and you want to do it - then do it. Thank you for seeing, 'Chained' - I'm so happy you enjoyed it - Heavens! - I'm half way thru another production already - I hope you will like this one too.

- To work now for, J.C.

November 21, 1935 -

Dear Madeline:
 It was nice of you to write to me about my recent radio broadcast. I am so glad you liked the play - and I thank you for the kind things you said about my reading.

- Best regards to you - Joan Crawford.

The radio broadcast mentioned was for the 'Lux Radio Theatre,' it aired on October 14, 1935. The sixty-minute broadcast was titled, *Within the Law* and was especially important to Joan because it was her first lengthy radio reading. She was relieved when it was over.

November 6th, 1935 -

Dear Mrs. Eddy:

 Thank you so much for expressing your sentiment toward Mr. Tone and myself with such a lovely card. We both greatly appreciate your good wishes for us.

- Sincerely, Joan Crawford.

The above-mentioned thank you would have been for a wedding card, congratulating Joan and her new husband, Franchot Tone, on their October 11th ceremony.

November 7, 1935 - To "Genie Chester."

Genie, darling -
It's a heavenly bowl; I have not millions of them. It's truly beautiful and you know by now how grateful I am to you for your thoughtfulness. I truly don't know when you find time to do the things you do.
Next time we come to New York we are going to take an apartment and live a quiet life and do things we want. We did so want to see your apartment and see you more often, but something happens in New York - I swear there only seems to be about four hours each day - then it's bed time - then up - then the shortest day again. You'll probably get your fill of me when I come in to do plays each year. But in the meantime, aren't you coming to our beautiful California? Dearest love and gratitude to you always, Genie.
- From, Joan.

December 30, 1935 - To "Genie Chester" of New York City - Handwritten, two-page letter on "Joan" imprinted stationary.

Genie Dear -
Where do you find such lovely things? - Your gift was wonderful. You should see the lovely golds and browns in my drawing room - the coloring is beautiful - Thank you from my heart. I hope you had a wonderful Christmas - Ours was - and it was made perfect by your present.
I'm hard at work on dance routines on the Clifton Webb picture - Today I danced from 9.00 AM till 2.00 PM - sitting down only long enough to put make up on. I'm so tired. I'm off to bed and it's only 7.30 PM.
- Goodbye for a little while, and deep love - Joan.

Interestingly, *Elegance,* the title of the Clifton Webb movie that Joan mentions rehearsing for in the above letter, was never made. The two stars clashed so often in rehearsals, the studio knew that even their best acting skills couldn't pull off the believable chemistry needed between their potential characters.

1936 - To "Genie Chester" of New York City - Handwritten letter on "JC" stationary -

Genie dear -
Sorry I've been so long in answering your sweet letter but I've been ill with the flu and a high fever. In bed for ten days. Your Christmas

in the country sounded enchanting. Where did you see that wonderful apartment you spoke of and how much was it? - We were ready to move in when you described it - really we were. Do you suppose it's dreadfully expensive?

I haven't gone to work yet - we can't find a story. Do write soon. If you see Douglas when he arrives, give him my best. And if you see Helen Hayes' play, tell me what you think of it. I'm heart sick I can't see her.

- Love from, Joan.

March 6, 1936 - To "Genie Chester" - A handwritten letter on name imprinted stationary. Her first name, "Joan," is printed on a slant, in the top left corner.

Genie, My Dear -

Sorry I have not answered your sweet letter before now - but I've been working three and four hours a day on my singing and reading scripts. I have not worked for four months. I called your sweet father and as you no doubt know, we saw him for one brief moment. Genie, he sent flowers and said, "now don't bother to write and thank me, as I know how busy you are."

Do please tell him I loved them, they are so beautiful. I promised him I would not thank him - so that's why I wish you'd tell him. We gave a reception to Stokowski, last Sunday. Over two hundred people arrived - it was really quite successful (I have no modesty). But Stokowski made it a huge success. He is so charming, do you know him?

Saw Douglas - I think he looks so well. No doubt you are seeing quite a lot of him by now.

- Best love to you - Joan.

A little background information on Genie Chester, whom many of these early thirties letters were written to. Genie was a friend of Douglas Fairbanks Jr., Joan came to know her as a result of her relationship and subsequent marriage to him, and even after their divorce, Joan maintained a regular correspondence with Genie. In many of her post Fairbanks divorce letters, Joan mentions seeing Doug, or asks Genie if she's seen him.

Genie's father was a highly successful businessman. She came from a wealthy family and as a result, she never worked, she didn't have to, she was independently wealthy and living off the family fortune. It is suspected that she had polio as a child, which crippled her, although her disability didn't stop her from mingling in high-class social circles.

In the above letter, Joan mentions Genie's father sending her the beautiful flowers. Joan became quite friendly with him. However, in a later letter, it's clear they had a falling out. As a result of this "argument" there is a definite strain in Joan's later relationship with Genie.

Their correspondence in the 1940's and 1950's is different, Joan apologizes a lot, for one reason or another, and it seems they haven't visited each other in a long time. Incidentally, Douglas Fairbanks Jr. maintained a life long friendship with Genie Chester. He evens mentions her in his autobiography, *Salad Days*.

April 11, 1936 -

Dear Madeline:
    It was most thoughtful of you to send me a card on my birthday. Thank you for thinking of me. Your photographic work is very good, I think. I enjoyed the pictures that came to me a month or so ago - and I suppose you took them. I am starting my new picture, 'The Gorgeous Hussy', in a few days, so I am pretty busy preparing for it.
        - Regards to you, Sincerely yours, Joan Crawford.

May 23, 1936 - On 'MGM' letterhead paper ~ in part...

    ...This is just a note as I'm getting ready to start, 'Gorgeous Hussy' and we have hundreds of costumes. Since you love music so much - I'm sorry you couldn't be here for the reception we gave for Stokowski - Even if Franchot and I did give it, it really was fun and I'm afraid quite successful. Stokowski drops by our house quite often, and we've had very interesting talks. Don't you envy me?
- More later, Love Joan.

May 23, 1936 - To "Genie Chester" of New York City - Handwritten letter on "Joan Crawford" imprinted stationary - A particularly interesting signature on this letter, she signs off as, "Joan Tone," her legal married name at the time.

Irmgard -
    This is just a note as I'm getting ready to start 'Gorgeous Hussy' - hundreds of costumes.
    Since you love music so much - I'm sorry you couldn't have been here for the reception we gave for Stokowski - Even if Franchot and I did give it, it really was fun and I'm afraid quite successful - Stokowski drops by our house quite often, and we've had some very interesting talks. Don't you envy me?
        - More later, Joan Tone.

A broodish portrait from *Paid* (1930).

The Gorgeous Hussy (1936) was the first film that Joan and new husband, Franchot Tone had made together since their marriage in 1935, but with Joan having a starring role and Franchot Tone having a mere 26 lines it caused a professional rivalry that spilled over into their marriage.

When Melvyn Douglas noticed Joan, Lionel Barrymore and Robert Taylor turning up to set each day with an army of their own hairdressers, make up artists, etc, etc. As a joke, he decided to turn up one day with some friends, family members, even a couple of dogs. Everyone was so used to this bizarre celebrity behavior being commonplace, no one on the set got his joke!

March 28, 1937

Dear Madeline,

It was really very generous of you to think of me on my birthday and I want to thank you for the good wishes in your telegram. I had expected to start another picture by this time, but it has been postponed for several weeks.

It is to be an adaptation of a story called MANNEQUIN, and of course I will have a chance to wear many gorgeous clothes. I am not sure who else will be in it. Write to me sometime and let me know how you are getting along.

- As ever, Joan Crawford.

April 18, 1937 -

Dear Helen,

My very best wishes to you on your marriage. I hope you will find great happiness. Thank you for remembering my birthday again this year. You have been very thoughtful.

Although I have a new picture scheduled to start some time next month, at present I am enjoying a vacation away from the studio, and I spend part of my time at home and part in the desert. The new film is to be THREE ROOMS IN HEAVEN, adapted from the story called MANNEQUIN. Good luck to you always - and thank you again for your kindness.

- As ever, Joan Crawford.

Mannequin had four working titles before finally settling on its original title. It was commonly referred to as, *Class, Saint or Sinner, Shop Girl* and *Three Rooms in Heaven.*

A pensive pose.

In *Conversations with Joan Crawford*, by Roy Newquist, Joan explains, or rather complains, about the script and even more so about her co-star, Spencer Tracy.

"'Mannequin' was a mistake all the way around; Spencer Tracy was so miscast he made an absolute muddle out of my part, which wasn't all that great to begin with. At first I felt honored to be working with Spence, and we even whooped it up a little bit off the set, but he turned out to be a real bastard. When he drank he was mean, and he drank all through production. He'd do cute things like step on my toes when we were doing a love scene - after he chewed on some garlic."

January 12, 1938

Dear Madeline,

Several days ago I arrived back home, and I brought your nice letter with me to answer from here. Of course, I know who you are. You have been one of my fans for a long time. And I know about your camera. About two years ago you took photographs of my so-called "Quins," and I saw the prints. As you say, you don't write very often - but I have received many cards and some telegrams. Thank you for the telegram you sent when I arrived in New York in December.

I appreciate the work you have done for the fan club, and I am sure Marian does, too. Write me again when you can. Good luck for the New Year!

- As ever, Joan Crawford.

January 25, 1938 - To "Genie Chester" of New York City - Handwritten letter on "JCT" (Joan Crawford Tone) stationary. The thank you given by Joan for Genie's sympathy note is a bit of a mystery here. She suffered no apparent human loss at this time in her life, so perhaps it was a note of sympathy for the loss of one of her beloved dogs...

Genie dearest -

Your sweet note of sympathy was a great comfort - Thank you so much for it and yesterday the blueprints and a letter from Mr. Crass. How good of you to remember - Franchot arrives home this week and we will go over it together - I've been working like mad ever since I returned. Three hours a day on my singing, then I ride my magnificent horse and practice polo an hour and a half each day - then I read a lot and the rest of the day and evening, the part of me that is "Craig's Wife" comes out and I wander around my heavenly home.

A busy day indeed! Just look at all of those signed photos.

(Spencer) *Tracy and I do "Anna Christie" on February seventh for Lux - If you care to listen. Do let me hear from you darling.*

- My dearest love to you - Joan.

March 31, 1938 - To "Genie Chester" of New York City - Handwritten letter on "JCT" stationary -

Genie dearest -

Your wire about "Anna Christie" and your letter about "Mannequin" made me so happy.

My new contract will be signed in a day or so, then I'm rushing on to New York for a week and while I'm on the train I shall study the plans of the apartment house you were so thoughtful to send me - and I'll attend to all that when I get there.

I've a week to spare, and as I missed some good plays, I'm coming in to catch up and I do hope we can see each other during this hectic trip. Did the baby arrive yet? - The suspense is awful!

- Love, Joan.

That new contract that Joan mentions in the above letter wasn't signed until May of 1938. MGM agreed to pay her $330,000 a year for five years. There was a limit totaling fifteen pictures, with no more than six productions in the first two years, and nine productions within the last three years.

November 27, 1938 - To "Genie Chester" of New York City. Typed letter on "426 North Bristol Avenue, West Los Angeles, California" stationary.

Genie dearest,

Please forgive me for not thanking you before this for your beautiful telegram about the broadcast, but making two pictures at once is no fun. "Shining Hour" overlapped, "Ice Follies" - I am skating like mad and singing like mad at the moment.

It looks as if I'll be working clear through Christmas and New Year's, but I hope to be in New York, the middle of January. I think of you often. Please write soon. and by the way, how is Fernie?

- My love to you, as ever - Joan

Joan performed six singing numbers for the *Ice Follies (1939)*. Four of those numbers were cut from the final print and the other two were re-dubbed. Joan announced her impending divorce from Franchot Tone during production.

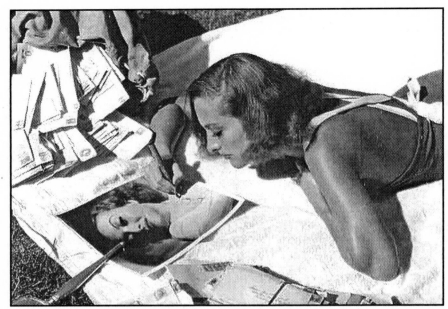
What better way to get through her fan mail than to sign photographs in the California sun.

By the look on Joan's face, this is a very serious letter.

In one of her most scathing critiques ever, Joan said - *"Christ. Everyone was out of their collective minds when they made Ice Follies. Me, Jimmy Stewart and Lew Ayres as skaters - preposterous. A dancer I am, a skater I'm not; whenever I couldn't fake it or use a double I skated on my ankles. Nice music and costumes, and the Shipstad ice people helped, but it was a catastrophe. The public thought so, too."*

January 4, 1939 - To "Genie Chester" of New York City - Handwritten letter on "Joan" imprinted stationary.

Genie dearest -
    The cigarette boxes are the loveliest I've ever seen - they look so heavenly in my drawing room. The enchanting teapot and packages of tea, had no card but they came in the same box as the cigarette boxes. I didn't know whether you'd sent them all or whether your mother of father had sent one. 'Ice Follies' still goes on - I hope to be released from the picture, retakes and all by the 15th of January. Then perhaps, on to New York.
    You know the apartment building you sent me the picture of? - Well, the apartment I wanted I gave up to Jean and her husband - they wanted it and my future with Franchot seemed all messed up. Jean is delighted with the apartment - so when I make my next trip, I'll look around for mine. I hope to see you soon and thank you for your wonderful Christmas gifts

- Joan.

April 15th, 1939 -

Dear Billy -
    Thank you so very much for your darling letter, I always enjoy hearing from you. I'm up to my neck in work at the moment. George (Cukor) has gathered a divine group of women for a movie about women, funnily enough to be called just that, 'The Women.'
    Norma Shearer, Rosalind Russell, Paulette Goddard, Joan Fontaine and I are all working like mad to make it the best picture possible. With George in command, we are being guided every step of the way. He's brilliant! It's long days, but I'm loving every minute of it so I always feel guilty for complaining that I need more sleep. We hope to be finished sometime in July, with the finished picture ready by the end of this year. I do hope you'll see it, Billy.

- Much love, Joan.

Frank Nugent of the *New York Times* had this to say about Joan's performance in *The Women (1939)*. *"Miss Crawford is as hard as nails in the Crystal Allen role, which is as it should be."*

George Cukor was labeled, 'The Women's Director' and in his film, aptly titled, *The Women*, he made sure he lived up to his reputation. There are an amazing number of female coincidences here. One hundred and thirty actresses were used in the film; the animals were all female and the artwork in the background of various scenes were all paintings of the female form.

No stand-ins were used in the fight scene where Rosalind Russell bites Paulette Goddard. The two women gave it their all. In fact, Russell's bite was so realistic it left a permanent scar on Goddard's arm.

An enormous studio success, *The Women*, was the second highest grossing film for MGM in 1939 - First place? - *Gone with the Wind.*

The Letters...1940's

"Did you know there were 25,000 baby girls christened with the name Joan this year? Half were named after me, and the others were named for Joan of Arc. Isn't that wonderful?"

- Joan Crawford (1940).

January 10, 1940 - To "Genie Chester" of New York City. A handwritten letter on 20th Century Fox Stationary. Envelope is stamped - "Special Delivery Airmail."

Genie Dearest -

Now that all the hectic rush is over, I can sit down and thank you profusely for my heavenly Christmas present. It's impossible to tell you how sweet the tea set looks in the cabinet, you have to see it. You look so well, do write soon and dearest love and a heartful of gratitude for your kindness -

- Joan.

January 31, 1940 - To "Genie Chester" of New York City, New York.

Genie, you angel -

As if you hadn't done enough. That flowered robe arrived and I nearly fainted. Of course I put it on her instantly - She looked beautiful in it. Thank you, thank you, thank you darling. I'm so happy that you can spend so much time with Victoria and Penelope, they are such a joy.
I'm sorry you will not be here this winter but I shall look forward to the summer when you will be here. I'm up to my neck in fittings and rehearsals for "Susan and God". It's very exciting but tiring so I'm off to bed -- Bless you darling, and write when you find the time.

- Much love - Joan and Cynthia

Joan sorts through her ever growing pile of mail.

Joan tending to her mail.

Who is Cynthia you may be wondering? - It is a little known fact that Christina, (about six months of age at the time of the above letter being written), was briefly named Cynthia, before Joan decided permanently on Christina. She was also known as Joan Jr. for a short time.

February 11, 1940

Dear Madeline:

Thank you very much for the good wishes you sent during the holidays. It has been a long time since I have had a letter from you. How has everything been going with you? Are you still doing photographic work? - Let me hear from you once in a while if you get time to write.

- My best to you, Joan Crawford.

This is a classic example of Joan communicating with her fans. Not only does she thank Madeline for her good wishes, she also remembers her line of work and even encourages her to write more often.

July 26, 1941 - To 'Sally Roberts' of New Rochelle, New York.

Dear Sally,

I was so happy to receive your sweet letter, and am sorry that I have taken so long in answering. Please try to understand that I would love to write longer and newsy letters, but my time is so limited at present that I feel fortunate in being able to devote as much time as this. however, I do love to read your letters and I hope that you will continue to write me.

The new picture, 'When Ladies Meet', is coming along very nicely, but I sometimes have to work ten or twelve hours a day, so you see it leaves very little time for personal correspondence. It makes me very happy to know that your friends liked 'A Womans Face', and you are sweet to take the time to tell me about it. I must close now. Please write again soon as I do love to hear from you.

- Love, Joan.

They All Kissed The Bride was released on July 31, 1942 - It was a role written for and already started by Carole Lombard but her untimely death in a plane crash during a war bond tour halted production.

Joan was loaned out by MGM for the very first time. She completed the film for Columbia Studios and donated her entire salary of $128,000 to the Red Cross, the organization responsible for the search and discovery of Lombard's body. She then fired her agent, Mike Levee, after finding out he took his usual ten percent commission on her salary.

One of Joan's youngest fans get his autograph wish from his favorite star.

Joan and Fred MacMurray in a scene from *Above Suspicion* (1943).

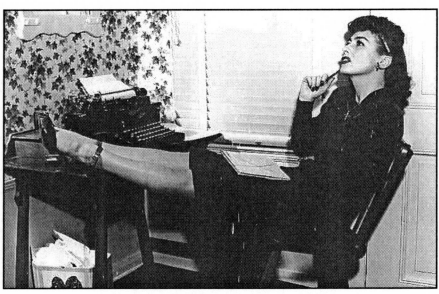

Joan thinks of what to say in her next letter.

October 31, 1941 - To "Sally," a particularly stern letter to a doubtful fan. Typed letter with handwritten postscript.

My dear Sally,

Your letter, too, was very enlightening. I did not realize, Sally, that I had to report to you, or any other fan who believes everything she reads in print.

I will tell you now, definitely, and if you don't believe me, there is nothing more I can do about it. I write all of my letters, if not actually in longhand, by the "hunt and peck" method on a typewriter. Mind you...I do not answer every letter I receive...that would be humanly impossible for anyone. I personally answer all the active members of my fan club, also the different fans and their friends who have been writing me over a period of years.

However, if everyone became as insistent, inquisitive, and such a "doubting Thomas" as you, I would indeed need many secretaries to answer all the questions.

Secondly, I do not understand what you mean when you wonder why my letter was mailed from New York. I see no reason why it shouldn't be mailed from New York since that's where I am. My dear Sally, did it ever occur to you that I have no choice in the selection of my pictures? I have a job, the same as you and any of your friends have, and do as I am told the way you must do in your job.

After two years of pleading, I was able to convince them that A WOMAN'S FACE would make a good picture. It happened I was lucky enough in winning that point, so please do not blame me for WHEN LADIES MEET.

I have no desire to be suspended, taken off salary, and let my children suffer merely because I refuse to do a picture such as WHEN LADIES MEET. I had no choice. So please, in the future, do not be so ready and willing to criticize us in the motion picture business.

Thank you for your good wishes, and I, too, hope that I will get some good pictures in the future. No one tries harder than I do, I'm quite sure.

- *Joan Crawford*

-

PS: I'm sure I'm not to blame if the State of California saw fit to change Brentwood to West Los Angeles, California, last year - J.C.

The following letter is particularly unusual in as much as it's written by Joan, for a then two and a half year old Christina. Written in a child like scrawl, she has gone to painstaking lengths to give the impression that Christina has written the letter herself. Since Genie

67

A vintage Maybelline cosmetics ad featuring a signed photo of Joan. She writes, "To Maybelline – The eye make-up I would never be without – Sincerely, Joan Crawford."

Chester was a close family friend, Joan undoubtedly sent the note from Christina's perspective, thinking it would be a cute gesture. It reads as follows:

December 29, 1941 - To "Genie Chester" of New York City, New York.

Dear Genie -
Thank you so much for my beautiful print done by the French child. I love it, it looks so pretty in my room, and my oh so lovely edition of 'The Wind In The Willows.' My mommie will only let me see it when I'm on her lap - she said it's too beautiful and we must take awful good care of it. You are so good to us. Please see us soon -
- Love, Christina.

October 16, 1942 - To "Genie Chester" of New York City - Handwritten letter on "JTC" notepaper -

Dearest, Gene -
At last the picture is completed. It lasted four months, that added to our marriage. There just hasn't been a moment. I never did thank you for the Christmas train gift. It was heavenly. It kept her busy which is so important on trains. I've thought of you, oh so much, knowing how happy you would be in my happiness. Oh, Genie, this sort of happiness I thought existed only in storybooks. It's perfection.
You must have had a glorious summer with all the children. How is your father? I haven't heard a word from any Chester for so long, yet I don't deserve to, as I've not written a line to anyone. I start work again in a week - do please write soon, Genie dearest.
- So much love, Joan.

An undated letter, written on "Christina" imprinted stationary, in Joan's hand.

Genie dearest -
My books are a treasure - and do you know something, my mother has never read them either, so you can imagine the fun the two of us are going to have reading them together. How wonderful you are to want me to have something that gave you so much joy when you were little. My mother has to write this for me but that does not mean I am not telling her what to write.
- All my love, Christina.

821 RESIDENCE OF JOAN CRAWFORD

BRENTWOOD HIGHLANDS, CALIFORNIA

ZA-H31

PS: That horrid mother of mine just informed me she's been so busy moving that she hasn't thanked you yet for my bath toys and swimsuit. Please accept my apology for my family.

January 1943 - To "Genie Chester" of New York City - Handwritten letter on "J.T.C" notepaper.

Genie, dearest -

How sweet, and wonderful and thoughtful you are. Christina adores her books. I've let her look at them and read parts of them, and on very special occasions she can have them on account of they are so lovely and I want her to take care of them. And you must know how I love my miniature cup and saucer; they look so sweet in the cabinet in the drawing room. Thank you, darling, for remembering us so handsomely.

Phillip (Terry) *and I had the most perfect Christmas any two people ever had in the world. Oh Genie, he is the most wonderful person, you will adore him. I can't wait till you meet him. Do write soon, it's too long in between letters and it's mostly my fault. I do hope you all received the plant and candy at Christmas, one just cannot depend on deliveries any more.*

- Love, Joan.

May 19, 1943 - To 'Sally Roberts' of Brooklyn, New York.

Dear Sally,

It was sweet of you to write to me and I'm so sorry that you haven't heard from me for quite some time. I've been terribly busy finishing up at the studio before my vacation and with my A.W.V.S nursery work and all; I just haven't had the time for letter writing.

How are you Sally? I do hope everything is running smoothly for you and that you are well and happy. We had planned to go to New York but have been unable to obtain reservations so will have to postpone the trip. So we will spend our vacation at home with our darling children. I imagine you've heard about our adopting little Phillip Terry II. He is just ten months old and has light hair and very blue eyes. He is such a little angel and I am sure you would love him if you could see him.

- Joan.

Joan's reference to 'finishing up at the studio' is no doubt referring to her role in, *Above Suspicion*. It was to be the last MGM/Joan Crawford film ever released. It appeared in theaters to mixed reviews on August 6th, 1943, but the media was speculating that the end of an eighteen-year business association was coming to an end. It is still unclear

A 1940s photo of Joan signed, "To Mary Kay. Thank you, from Joan Crawford."

if Joan quit MGM or if she was let go, whatever the case may be, she wasn't unemployed for long. A too good to refuse $500,000 salary for a three picture deal was offered to her by Warner Brothers, however, her joy at joining a new studio was short lived.

The all star war time morale booster, *Hollywood Canteen* was Joan's first time out with her new studio, after only a week of shooting, she became so upset with her minor role that she demanded to be taken off salary until they found a *real* picture for her. On remembering her experience on the picture she said, *"A very pleasant pile of shit for the wartime audience, but forget that I even appeared in it. I don't think I did."*

Warner's listened to her concerns, with their main aim to now find 'the picture' to introduce their new star, but with director Michael Curtiz having his heart set on Barbara Stanwyck for his new big picture, the down time at Warner's was becoming increasingly frustrating for her. When Joan's name came up as a possibility, director, Michael Curtiz, flew into a rage, yelling, *"Me direct that temperamental bitch! - Not on your goddamn life!"*

Joan had a fight on her hands so she did something that no established actor does, ever! - She swallowed her pride and went back to basics...submitting herself to a screen test! It was the only way she knew how to convince Curtiz that the part belonged to her. She convinced him and he agreed that Joan Crawford *was, Mildred Pierce.* It was *Mildred Pierce* who gave Joan Crawford her only Oscar for Best Actress. For Joan, it was a career high, a new beginning. Joan Crawford was far from washed up.

The success of the film forced Curtiz to compliment Joan on her performance, and her professionalism, *"When I agreed to direct Miss Crawford, I felt she was going to be as stubborn as a mule and I made up my mind to be plenty hard on her. Now that I've learned how sweet she is, I take back even thinking those things about her."*

Upon her divorce from Phillip Terry in 1946, Joan customarily changed the name of her Brentwood Estate and every toilet seat in the house. However, she went to a whole new extreme this time, even renaming her son! - At the age of four, Phillip Terry Jr., was given a new identity, he was now known as, 'Christopher Crawford.'

June 30, 1943.

Dear Sally,

Thank you for your sweet letter and how nice to hear from you again. Yes, I was terribly disappointed in not being able to make the trip to New York with so many good plays there this season but we have decided

73

Candid shots of Joan with her fans.

to postpone the trip until early fall since it has been impossible to obtain reservations. I'm so glad to hear that I'm not missing much because of the weather being so terrifically hot there.

Phillip Terry II certainly is adorable and you were sweet to say that he is lucky to have our love and guidance. Of course, it's going to be dreadfully hard to give your husband to 'Uncle Sam' but when you think of all the others who have had to give theirs up too and many who have sons and husbands 'over there', it shouldn't be so hard to do. Do send the picture of you and Bob. I'd love to have it. Please write again soon,

- As ever, Joan.

October 13, 1943 - To a friend in Ohio - 'in part'...

I was unable to go along on the Bond Tour. I'm glad you saw and liked 'Above Suspicion.' Yes, Christina is a year older than Roger. She is four – and is now going to school full days. Thank you for your good wishes on my 'new venture with Warner Bros.' My first picture will be 'Night Shift,' adapted from a novel of the same title.

Joan eventually turned down the role in *Night Shift*. It was originally offered to Ann Sheridan, however it was postponed indefinitely before eventually being offered to Joan. Once rejected by her it was scrapped completely.

January 12, 1944 - To "Genie Chester" of New York City, New York.

Another hand written letter to family friend, Genie Chester, on behalf of a then four and a half year old Christina, entirely in Joan's hand. Written on kiddie notepaper, with a clown and boy and girl animated characters at the top of the page, Joan writes for Christina, again...

Dearest Aunt Genie -

Mommie said she wrote one note already thanking you for my "Birds Christmas Carol" but I love it so I wanted her to write again. It's so beautiful - Thank you oh so much for remembering me at Christmas and I hope to see you soon.

- Love, Christina.

Joan mingles with her fans and signs autographs.

January 20, 1944 - To "Genie Chester" of New York City - Handwritten letter on "J.T.C" stationary.

Genie dearest -

Just a hurried note to say I'm busier than hell. No cook - no nurse and part of the housework to do. I'm on the go from 6.00 AM till 11.00 PM. Please say hello to Douglas for me, tell him I wrote a very long letter in answer to his last one a year ago - one he never answered - ask him if her ever received it, please.

Christina and Phillip (aka Christopher) *both had chicken pox, recovered very well from that, then came down with the flu - but all is well again now. Don't work too hard, darling. Take care of yourself, and write soon to your devoted...*

- Joan.

August 22nd, 1944 - Typed letter signed in full.

Dear Dorothy,

It was so nice hearing from you again after all these months and I'm sorry you didn't drop me a note while you were here. I'm getting ready to start "Mildred Pierce" the first of September and am going to the studio for story conferences almost daily.

Yes, Christina is a "big girl" now and I certainly do know what you mean when you say children take up a lot of your time. I'm returning the snapshot to you as I thought you might want it for your album. I hope you won't wait so long before writing again to -

-   Joan Crawford

PS: I'm sending you a photo under separate cover, which I hope you will like.

December 12th, 1944 - To Clifton Webb at "The Park Lane Hotel" - NYC.

Clifton dear,

I didn't have your New York address but, after mailing everyone in town, finally tracked it down. I wanted to tell you that everyone is talking about how magnificent you are in "LAURA." We hope to run it on Saturday night and are so excited at the prospect. Am terribly sorry to hear that you've been ill since you returned to New York and hope that this finds you your own self again. Deepest love to you and Mabel and may you have a beautiful holiday.

- Joan and Phillip (Terry).

426 NORTH BRISTOL AVENUE
WEST LOS ANGELES, 24 CALIFORNIA

August 22nd, 1944.

Dear Dorothy:

It was so nice hearing from you
again after all these months and I'm sorry
you didn't drop me a note while you were
here.

I'm getting ready to start "Mildred
Pierce" the first of September and am going
to the studio for story conferences almost
daily.

Yes. Christina is a "big girl" now
and I certainly do know what you mean when
you say children take up a lot of your time.

I'm returning the snapshot to you
as I thought you might want it for your album.

I hope you won't wait so long before
writing again to -

Joan Crawford

Dorothy M. Petersen,
734 Giddings Ave., S.E.
Grand Rapids, 6, Michigan.

P.S. I'm sending you a photograph, under
separate cover, which I hope you will like.

J.C.

No visible date, but the year is 1945 - To "Genie Chester" of New York City - Handwritten letter on filigree trimmed paper.

Genie dearest -
I'm so glad you liked the little thought for Christmas and happy that Vicky liked hers too. How nice that she is with your mother and Dodo (Douglas Fairbanks Jr). Working again is marvelous but a bit tiring, the hours are from 5.00 AM, till 7.30 PM, then there is the bath - makeup off - dinner - hair to dress and dry - study - to bed, if I'm lucky by eleven!
But it's worth it, as I believe we have a good one. The year and a half waiting for them right story has been worth waiting for. Don't work too hard, darling with your war work, and please find time to write to your devoted, Joan, who sends you all her love.

The movie that Joan mentions waiting a year and a half for, is none other than, *Mildred Pierce*, although she's complaining about her tiresome work schedule, she no doubt forgot all about that when she won the Best Actress Oscar for her performance.

December 26, 1945 - To "Genie Chester" of New York City - Handwritten letter with a stamp of a dog scratching his ear and "Joan" underneath it as the letterhead.

Genie dearest -
Hope you had a lovely Christmas - I adored my gift, and it would have done your heart good to have seen the children with your gifts. Mary Poppins comes back - Penny - Mother Goose and the figures of Mary Poppins and Penny are enchanting. Thank you for all of us, we are so grateful for making our Christmas such a happy one.
The news about Phillip and me probably shocked you, there is so much to tell you when we meet, that can't be written. My dearest love and I long to visit with you, however it must wait for a few months.
- Ever, Joan.

It's interesting to note how Joan mentions her break up with Phillip Terry in this letter. She very cleverly avoids going into full details, not wanting to write anything down, just in case it got into the wrong hands.

March 1946 - A handwritten note card with a 'J.T.C' (Joan Terry Crawford) letterhead, to gossip columnist, Hedda Hopper, after being awarded her Best Actress Oscar for *Mildred Pierce*.

Joan with her beloved dachshund's, Pupsen and Baby. Despite Baby originally being Franchot Tone's dog, she got full custody and kept both dogs together long after their divorce.

A playful mother/daughter game. Joan with Christina in happier times.

Hedda Dear,

Over a year ago you wrote in your column that I'd win the award - You were so helpful and encouraging. May I say I'm deeply grateful.

- Joan.

March 22, 1946 - Handwritten letter to "Genie Chester" of New York City, New York.

Genie Dearest,

Your letter was sweet - I'm still on Cloud Seven as far as the "Oscar" is concerned. I've talked to Charles a few times and I believe he will be out here in about two or three weeks - It will be nice to see him again.

This is being written on the set, so forgive the briefness of it. I expect to finish in about two weeks and then either come to New York or go to a ranch with the children. However, I'll let you know definitely.

- Dearest love, always - Joan.

Joan writes the above note shortly after her Oscar win for Best Actress, in *Mildred Pierce*. The movie set she refers to writing the letter from is, *Humoresque* (1946).

Humoresque is a remake of the 1920 film of the same name. The original title of this 1946 version was, *Rhapsody In Blue. Humoresque* was so popular in Mexico, it played continually for three years, in the same theater. After a screening of *Humoresque* in Joan's private home theater, John Garfield offered to carry Christina up to bed. She was mesmerized by him, *"I decided,"* she said in her book, *Mommie Dearest, "that if I ever I married, it would have to be someone like him."* Christina is twice divorced.

Despite their on screen chemistry and box office success, *Humoresque* was the only time John Garfield and Joan were teamed together. His long-term heart problems and untimely death at age 39, in 1952, saw the biggest attendance at a movie stars' funeral since silent screen heartthrob, Rudolph Valentino.

September 2, 1947 - To "Genie Chester" of New York City - Handwritten letter on "J.T.C" notepaper.

Genie, darling -

The sweater was heavenly - Thank you for thinking of us. I forgot to enclose a picture in the last letter, but here is one taken when they first

Joan is mobbed as she exits the Ritz.

Joan happily signs an oversized portrait of herself for one of her devoted fans.

arrived. They are twins but as you see, not identical. I cannot tell the press they are twins as they are too easily traced.

Tina returned from six weeks of camp so I took her and Christopher away for a week, that's why I haven't written - I leave for Honolulu by myself the 19th of September - for a much needed rest. I'll be gone 16 days. Do write my dearest love.

- Joan.

The above letter was written barely a month after Joan adopted the twins, Cynthia and Cathy. Her initial fear of not letting the press know they were twins didn't last too long, as it was public knowledge she had adopted twin girls soon after bringing them home.

September 18, 1947 - To "Genie Chester" of New York City - Handwritten letter on "J.T.C" stationary. Again, Joan is slow in getting rid of her stationary with her previous husbands initials on it. She filed for divorce from Phillip Terry on March 12, 1946. Here, over a year later, she is still sending out the "J.T.C" letterhead -

Darling, Genie -

I sent Mrs. Eastman a check for one hundred dollars; do you suppose that was alright?

Yes, darling, I did know Douglas and Mary Lee are expecting a baby and did you know that Charles and Ruth are expecting another one?

Speaking of babies...my angels and Cynthia and Cathy - the latter being the one with all the hair. How interesting about Mademoiselle. Please tell her when she gets settled here to let me know her address because I may want her for sewing.

Larsen and I leave tomorrow - Golly, I shall miss the children so much, but I do need a rest. I got none last winter if you recall. I'll be at the Royal Hawaiian (can't even spell I'm so tired) for sixteen days, and then home.

- Love, Joan.

August 29, 1949 - To Katherine Le Blanc, a fan living in Corona, New York.

Dear Katherine -

It was nice to receive your letter and a new picture of the children. I can just picture how proud you must be of three boys. It is always a thrill to see our own little ones preform, so it was without any trouble I could almost feel the joy you experienced.

Always smiling, always signing. Joan would never say no to an autograph request.

The twins have had a summer full of fun and keeping busy. They not only learned to scale the back fence but found much enjoyment in taking swimming lessons. The two older ones were away at summer camps. I visited Christina and was so pleased to find the wonderful camp and time she was having. They are both home now and we are rushing madly to get ready for school. We seem to thrive on all this excitement.

I do appreciate your loyalty over so many years. It always gives me an incentive to work harder than ever to provide more entertainment for those who find enjoyment in my work. The best of everything to you and your family.

- Sincerely yours, Joan Crawford.

The Letters...1950's

Lyn Markham - (Joan) -
"I wouldn't have you if you were hung with diamonds upside down!"
                                        - Female On The Beach (1955).

March 13th, 1952 - Mrs. Ruth Emerson, Van Nuys, California.

Dear Mrs. Emerson,
        Thank you so much for your nice letter. I am deeply sorry to know that your life has been upset recently. It is a hard adjustment to make when a home is broken and there are children in it.
        I think it is fortunate that your children are old enough to allow you the freedom necessary to start a career. I feel it is essential at a time like this to keep busy with something you are most interested in.
        You ask if you are too old to go back to studying dramatics. I do not think anyone is too old to study, and I do not consider 39 old. Nowadays a woman can keep herself attractive and young looking. Naturally, it will take time to make the readjustment, but I am sure you will find the happiness you seek if you go about it with courage and determination. I hope I have helped you a little, and do write to me again and let me know how you are getting along.
                                        - Sincerely, Joan Crawford.

May 18, 1952 - Typed letter, on "Hampshire House," New York City stationary - To "Miss Gertrude Walker" of Beverly Hills, California.

Gertrude, dear -
        Your letter was forwarded on to me in New York. Darling, I hate to say that I no longer maintain those rooms in the Hollywood Hospital. However, if your friend can have his doctor speak to Dr. Wm E. Branch,

426 NORTH BRISTOL AVENUE
LOS ANGELES 24, CALIFORNIA

April 14, 1951

Katherine LeBlanc
103-10 -- 35th Avenue
Corona, New York

Dear Katherine,

It is with a deep feeling of gratefulness that I wish to thank you for the beautiful birthday card. Each year I find this day so full of happiness because of the thoughtfulness of my many friends. It was so sweet of you to remember me as you always do on all special occasions.

The friendly greeting and your personal note gave me joy. I spent part of the day opening gifts, cards and letters. Being so near to Easter, and having had such a marvelous day with the children, I found myself left with the most pleasant memories of two wonderful days.

I have found that one's life is enriched by the loyalty and sincerity of friends. I feel I am most fortunate in sharing so much richness with so many true and wonderful friendships.

Best of wishes and good luck to you always.

Sincerely yours,

JOAN CRAWFORD

who is one of the heads of Hollywood Presbyterian, and I am sure Dr. Branch will be able to do something to help him.

I just received your note and I am answering it immediately. Even if it doesn't get there before the operation, have him still speak to Dr. Branch. Thank you darling for all the sweet things you said, and we must get together when I return, which will be around, June 7th or 8th.

- Joan.

December 4, 1952 - To an unidentified Illinois movie reviewer about the upcoming Academy Awards ceremony - In part.

I agree with you completely that Jane Froman should be recognized and a special Oscar given to her, not only for her voice and touch in 'With A Song In My Heart' - she has my Oscar for her great courage.

Thank you for working on your 'Crusade for Crawford', I'm sure I haven't a chance. From all I hear, Shirley Booth will get the award this year, and I believe it couldn't happen to a nicer human being or a greater actress.

Forgive me for running and cutting this letter short, but I have no cook and no help at all and there are so many chores for me to get at, house, marketing, menus, children and a little thing called a career.

In 1953, Joan corresponded with a 'Clifford W. Benson' of the "American Iris Society" in Saint Louis, Missouri. It is unknown how long their written correspondence lasted, but in the year of 1953, Joan wrote a letter to Cliff each and every month.

January 6, 1953 - To 'Clifford W. Benson' of the 'American Iris Society.'

My dear Cliff Benson,

I'm so terribly sorry but your letter and the slides got mixed up in the Christmas mail and I'm sorry to say that I just didn't get to it till now, or see it till now. I do hope you'll forgive my seeming rudeness.

How sweet you were to go ahead on the blue. It is a fabulous color. The # 52-3A is the most delicate shade of blue I've ever seen. The other blue that you sent the slide of has more purple in it according to your slide. No wonder you had so many compliments. It is silver-blue, delicate...rich.... and beautiful. And what a great compliment it is to have you name it the 'Joan Crawford Iris'. I'm so deeply grateful to you. I'm sure you know that. You speak of a black iris. It sounds fascinating and it must look very tropical and beautiful.

90

Joan makes one of her younger fans very happy by using his back as a surface to sign her name.

Of course it didn't bore me to read all your quotes. How proud you must be. I'm glad you went ahead with the color you picked for me. Your choice was perfect. Of course you can have my permission for a white iris named 'Cliquot'. I'll send you pictures of my children in case you'd like to name any after them. The babies are very dark eyed and have dark brown hair. They're French and Irish, like I am. Only I came out with the blue eyes and they came out with the brown. Chris is a Viking with blue eyes and blonde hair and so is Tina. Bless you - and a happy New Year to you, and thank you for your friendship and for your interest in me. I'm so deeply grateful.

- Joan Crawford.

It's fairly obvious that Clifford Benson was a flower grower who was creating new strains of iris and naming them after various members of Joan's family. Even 'Cliquot,' Joan's beloved poodle had a white iris created and named in his honor.

January 12, 1953 - Typed letter to "Genie Chester" of New York City -

Genie, darling,

Thank you so much for your lovely Christmas card. How good it was to hear from you. The only sad part in my life is that we have lost touch with each other as far as correspondence is concerned. I'm sure we could never lose touch with each other as far as our friendship and our spirits go. Our friendship has been on too sound a basis for anything to happen to it.

Is there any chance of your coming to California? - I certainly will not make another trip to New York without letting you know in advance. Of course, my last two were purely business and it was very hectic. If you read the papers, you must have seen that I was there on personal appearances and working like a dog.

I do hope you saw "Sudden Fear," and if you did, I hope you liked it as it's one of my pets. Happy New Year to you, darling. My dearest love to you for a very happy '53. And give my love to your Father for me.

- As ever, your very devoted, Joan.

January 22, 1953 - To "Dore Freeman" c/o MGM Studios - Typed letter on her imprinted "426 Bristol Avenue, California" stationary.

Dore, darling:

Please forgive this very belated note - but it's impossible to go into detail and tell you how busy I've been - what with the illness of the

Joan would choose new stationary every year, or every husband, whichever came first.

Joan happily meets her fan club and signs autographs

children, the auction going on on Wilshire Blvd - virus hitting the whole house...but anyway - I'm sure you understand.

Thank you for your good wishes - your sweetness - your thoughtfulness, and for sending me the foreign magazines. How good you are to me. The telephone number is Arizona 7-9991. Bless you, dear - and may the New Year bring you everything your heart desires is the wish of your very devoted.

- Joan.

January 28, 1953 - Typed letter to "Genie Chester" of New York City -

Genie darling,

I'm delighted you're coming out. My house is in an awful uproar at the moment. I'm redecorating and redoing. Have you ever known me when I wasn't? Darling, my telephone number is Arizona 8-4279. Do, please, call me the moment you get to town. I can't wait to see you and, of course, I can't wait to see your mother and father, too. But you, especially.

You'll find many changes - and you'll love my children. I think you, more than anyone in the world, will see what I've tried to do in these four children. I'm sending this airmail special so you'll get it before you leave. I love you very much and I've missed you. Can't we have a night - just with the kids and me - so you can see them? God bless you, darling. You have the number, you have the address and you have a very special place in my heart.

- Joan.

February 18, 1953 - To Clifford W. Benson of the 'American Iris Society.'

My Dear Cliff,

Thank you so much for your cards to Chris, your letter to me and the photographs. Incidentally, you were in such a hurry, you forgot to sign your letter. Of course, I understand about your being out of town and working. God forbid, too, that there'll ever be another war, whether you're in the Air Force or now -- just God forbid there be another war.

I'm sorry you were in L.A. and I didn't know about it, we would have gotten together. By the way, the pictures of my family and me - we haven't had a chance to all get together. Either the big kids are home and the little ones at school or vice versa.

You ask about the other children's names: Christina is 13; Christopher is 10; and the twins are 6. Their names are Cynthia and Cathy. Yes, not only am I French and Irish - but so are the twins. Now I know that you are French and Danish - with a little Norwegian thrown in for good measure.

94

February 18, 1953

My Dear Cliff:

Thank you so much for your cards to Chris, your letter to me and the photographs. Incidentally, you were in such a hurry, you forgot to sign your letter.

Of course, I understand about your being out of town and working. God forbid, too, that there'll ever be another war, whether you're in the Air Force or now -- just God forbid there be another war.

I'm sorry you were in L.A. and I didn't know about it. Had I known, we would have gotten together. By the way, the pictures of my family and me - we haven't had a chance to all get together. Either the big kids are home and the little ones at school or vice versa. You ask about the other children's names: Christina is 13; Christopher is 10 and the twins are 6. Their names are Cynthia and Cathy.

Yes, not only am I French and Irish - but so are the twins. Now I know that you're French and Danish - with a little Norwegian thrown in for good measure.

I can't wait to hear about your experiences with the ballet. Yes, it will be good to reminisce. Thank you for your sweet wishes for my family and me. I'll get the photographs to you soon and I can't wait for your photographs.

Thank you for your good wishes, too, on the Oscar. Yes, I understand, too, that the entire proceedings will be televised. However, since I just work here, I don't know much about it. We never do until we get there.

Please forgive the brief note, but I'm rushing off to a conference on the picture. I hope to see and hear from you soon.

God bless.

JOAN CRAWFORD

Clifford W. Benson
Region 18, American Iris Society
1201 Verl Place
St. Louis 14, Mo.

I can't wait to hear about your experience with the ballet. Yes, it will be good to reminisce. Thank you for your sweet wishes for my family and me. I'll get the photographs to you soon and I can't wait for your photographs. Thank you for your good wishes, too, on the Oscar. Yes, I understand, too, that the entire proceedings will be televised. However, since I just work here, I don't know much about it. We never do until we get there.

Please forgive the brief note, but I'm rushing off to a conference on the picture. I hope to see and hear from you soon.

- God bless - J.C.

The year, 1953 was the first year that the Academy Awards were televised. The thank you for the Oscar wishes is for Joan's nomination for Best Actress in *Sudden Fear*. Ironically, her rival, Bette Davis, was nominated in the same category for her performance in, *The Star*. Both actresses went home empty handed. The gold statue for Best Actress went to Shirley Booth for her role in, *Come Back, Little Sheba*.

If losing the Oscar was disappointing, Joan's final salary on *Sudden Fear* made the loss a little easier to bear. The terms of her contract was one of Joan's most lucrative business moves to date. After agreeing to a deal that gave her fifty per cent of the film profits, her base salary of $240,000 was only a small percentage of her final paycheck. By the time *Sudden Fear* had finished its theatrical run, Joan's paycheck had jumped to a whopping one million dollars!

March 3, 1953 - To Clifford W. Benson of the 'American Iris Society.'

Dear Cliff,

Oh, how you must of known I'd adore the precious poodle pictures and how sweet and charming you were to send them. Aren't they wonderful little characters? The Hula dancer, the little hearts and flowers, Valentine 'Babette', and how many times have you seen little boys that look just like Tempo. The 'Can-Can' dancer and the dainty ballerina...and I don't know if Suzy who was chosen 'king' is enjoying her role of 'The Clown' - she looks like she'd be more comfortable doing Shakespeare.

Oh, the smiles - well I'll admit to audible chuckles over this and I can't wait to show them to the children, but I'm saving it for a time when we can all sit down and laugh together. I'm showing this at the moment to my Cliquot who just tells me he thinks Coquette is a girl he knew in Salt Lake City, but I think not, since Coquette's from Richmond Heights.

Oh, Cliff - I don't know when anything has delighted me so. And when I came home from the studio and found the poodles, I just relaxed all

Joan poses with a group of young fans.

over and took my sweet time enjoying them. Thank you again for being
very sweet to...

- Joan Crawford.

This letter is particularly interesting as it shows the very close relationship that Joan had with her dog at the time, a white poodle, named Cliquot. It's seems Cliff has included some photographs of other poodles, all dressed up in various costumes. In a strange and more than likely 'alcohol induced' moment, she even mentions what Cliquot thinks of one particular poodle that she's showing him!

Cliquot, led a charmed life. He dined on food that most humans would only dream of having on special occasions. His main diet consisted of white meat chicken and ground sirloin and for dessert he would have his choice of ice-cream flavors, washed down with a little ginger ale.

He wore custom made outfits from Hammacher Schlemmer, usually a red jacket with a black collar, complete with a monogrammed 'CC' - A heart shaped pocket would carry a Kleenex, just in case he had to blow his nose and on more formal occasions he would be seen out and about wearing his customized rhinestone collar.

March 17, 1953 - Typed letter to "Genie Chester" of New York City.

Genie, my darling -
There just are no words to tell you how deeply I regret not having seen you again while you were in our town. It's been so long since you've been here - I tried to tell Flobelle about how I tried to reach you several times, but either the line was busy, you were out, or doing this or that - and my studio hours, as you know, are - well, they're not very accurate or dependable. I'm sure you understand that.

I've never worked so hard in my life, trying to keep my head above water and my name in the papers. You see, our picture was released too early, actually, for people to remember it Academy-Award wise and then we had to start the whole publicity campaign over again and at the same time I was trying to move into Paramount and then a new picture came up at Metro that I want very much to do. And even though you know you can't push - you still do. At least I do.

I felt so badly that I had the - not argument - but discussion with your father that night and questioned him on the subject he was on. You know, I find that people like your father very often take on a job that will keep them very busy and get them out of town just to have an activity, because they don't want to face the daily things in life that surround them. I know that I can say this to you home-wise, I know that even I, with my lovely home, (which unfortunately was terribly torn up when you were

*here, with carpenters, painters, etc.) even I, every now and then, just say,
"I can't take it any more." And I want to run away just to a motel where I
can be quiet with no phones -- nothing.*

*I believe too, that Helen Hayes in order to get away from the death
of Mary took "Mrs. McThing" which is so unworthy of her - but she is so
completely immersed in it that she thinks it's the greatest play in the world.
But that's only because it takes her on the road - on tour - away from her
home.*

*She wrote me once, very recently, that she was delighted to be
away from all the turmoil of the activities of daily routine and she said,
"As long as I'm there, I feel guilty if I don't take care of things, but once
I'm on the road -- oh, how quickly you can forget...." and I know what she
means.*

*You see, that's why I questioned your father, because I knew that
one day - and one day soon, one of the business men that he's going to ask
for a contribution will question him and say, "Well - so we pay for medical
students and for their education. But what is the percentage out of ten that
really make good doctors, and why should we pay $10,000 for bad medical
students - or bad doctors?"*

*This is the question I brought up that he couldn't answer, but he
was still willing to get the hell out and get on tour -- or "hit the road", as
we say. I know you know what I mean, but I shouldn't have argued with
him about it. I should have let it lay. It was joy enough to see you and your
father and your mother - without causing any dissension.*

*All I know is that I was very sad that I was in story conferences
from early morning until late at night at one studio, then rushing over to
another to be even later at night over there. Please understand. Please say
you'll forgive me. It's my loss, actually, that I didn't get to see you.*

*Just know that I love you and miss you very much and that you
hold a very warm and great spot in my heart. You always have and you
always will. Let me know what your plans are. It seems I won't be in New
York for quite a long time if my present plans materialize, but I'm hoping
you'll come back out here one day soon. My house will be in order very
soon and we could see each other and have our long, good, wonderful
talks again. It's been too long, but never for a moment has my love not
been with you.*

- Joan.

March 19, 1953 - Typed letter to "Dore Freeman" of MGM Studios -

Dore dear -
*What an angel you were to come over last night. I don't have to
tell you that I always feel so safe when I know you're here and the children*

99

always light up when I tell them you're coming to visit, have dinner, whatever.

I was just sorry we didn't have time to visit - but that's comin' up when I get settled - back home again in Culver City. Thank you again, honey.

- With love, as ever - Joan.

March 26, 1953 -

Bettina Darling:
Oh my - oh my - oh my! - I love my mukluks - I was just fine, then I happened to pick up that exquisitely beautiful mirror and looked into it without lipstick --or anything -- I happened to look into the good part.

I turned it over, saying, "Isn't it beautiful?" and I got a magnified view of me that scared the B'Jesus out of me! - When I'm made up, it won't scare me as much - It'll scare me a little, but not quite so much.

And you, of course, with that eagle-eye of yours, Bettina, knew that my little hand mirror in my make-up kit was broken - cracked beyond repair on one side. Darling, let's hope that this will bring me luck. Not for an Oscar - I don't mean that...But let's hope this mirror will bring me luck. I want you to carve something on the handle of it, or around the rim, so that I'll always have your signature in front of me. I'll always know that you gave it to me - that's very easy to remember, but thank you, thank you, thank you. Now - If I can only remember not to look in the wrong side. And, unless I put lipstick on, any side could be the wrong side.

My mukluks will keep me warm, my carpets clean - my feet lovely...and I must keep myself lovely in order to look in that lovely, exquisite mirror you gave me. And, Betty, forgive me for digressing for a moment, but you are a real dream girl helping me so much. I can't tell you how happy I am - my address book in such perfect condition. Poor darling, on your weekend doing nothing but signing those envelopes and getting everything in order for me - for autographing - what an angel you are! - I can only offer you at the moment my deepest friendship - my warmest devotion, my deepest curtsy and my heart and extended hand.

- Bless you - Joan.

April 9, 1953 - Typed letter to "Genie Chester" of New York City.

Genie, darling -
I was delighted with your letter. Of course I knew you understood and yet I felt so terrible guilty. I do hope you'll be back here soon. I'm glad you saw Douglas when he was there a few weeks ago. Sorry he was

100

426 NORTH BRISTOL AVENUE
LOS ANGELES 49. CALIFORNIA

April 9, 1953

My Dear Clifford Benson:

How can I begin to thank you for the exquisitely beautiful purple iris you sent me for my birthday. How sweet and thoughtful you were to remember me so beautifully. And I suppose I should have known I would get such supremely beautiful iris - if you sent them. I've just never seen any so lovely.

Please forgive my seeming rudeness in not writing you sooner, but I'm at MGM rehearsing my next picture, a musical entitled "Why Should I Cry" in which I'll sing and dance. They've had me in dance rehearsals every day between 5-6 hours and in between that I've been holding conferences with the director of my next picture "Lisbon" (which will follow immediately at Paramount in June). After that I'll go to Republic for my first western - "Johnny Guitar". Isn't that an exciting schedule? I know I'm lucky to have three pictures to do in a row. I hope you'll like them all - I'm trying very hard to make them good.

Thank you so very much again, for being so sweet, wonderful, thoughtful and generous to a deeply grateful and devoted

JOAN CRAWFORD

Clifford W. Benson
American Iris Society
1201 Verl Pl.
St. Louis 14, Mo.

ill with the virus, however. Next time you write him, give him my love, will you?

Incidentally, I'm afraid to even talk about your father - he's probably not speaking to me. You might tell him I'm still his friend anyway - even though I did criticize him a bit. He's done that to me all my life; so give me a crack at it - huh? Tell him that for me, will you? Thank you for saying, "I love you and always understand when your time is taken up by work." - I'm at Metro rehearsing my next picture, a musical entitled, "Why Should I Cry?"

It was pushed up ahead of "Lisbon" (which I'll do next). I'm dancing 5-6 hours a day and it's a little rugged, but wonderful fun. The musical will be in color and I'll sing and dance -- so you can imagine how exciting it is. Right after that I'll rush over to Paramount for "Lisbon", and follow that immediately with a western, "Johnny Guitar." Busy girl? You bet - but lucky.

My love to you always. And if there's the slightest chance you might be here, please let me know - how I'd love to see you.

- Joan.

April 9, 1953 - To 'Clifford W. Benson.'

My Dear Clifford Benson -
How can I begin to thank you for the exquisitely beautiful purple iris you sent me for my birthday. How sweet and thoughtful you were to remember me so beautifully. And I suppose I should have known I would get such supremely beautiful iris - if you sent them. I've just never seen any so lovely.

Please forgive my seeming rudeness in not writing to you sooner, but I'm at MGM rehearsing my next picture, a musical, entitled, 'Why Should I Cry', in which I'll sing and dance. They had me in dance rehearsals every day between 5-6 hours and in between that I've been holding conference with the director of my next picture, 'Lisbon', (which will follow immediately at Paramount in June.) After that I'll go to Republic for my first western, 'Johnny Guitar.' Isn't that an exciting schedule? I know I'm lucky to have three pictures to in a row. I hope you like them all - I'm trying very hard to make them good.

Thank you so very much again, for being so sweet, wonderful, thoughtful and generous to a deeply grateful and devoted.

- Joan.

This letter shows just how busy 1953 was for Joan. Two of the three pictures mentioned were made and as usual, there were some interesting behind the scenes antics going on. Despite the lowly budget,

102

A signed photo to a fan. Joan was in her early fifties in this photograph.

Joan liked the script of *Why Should I Cry* so much she agreed to a pay cut to make the picture and accepted her $125,000 salary in a stretched out eighty-three installments, in order to lessen her taxes for that year. The film was released on October 13, 1953 and renamed, *Torch Song.*

In the next letter dated, June 6, 1953, Joan refers to the film as *Torch Song* and explains how difficult her final scenes were. This was Joan's comeback film for MGM and on her first day on set she was treated like a returning Queen. In anticipation of her arrival, a huge banner reading, 'WELCOME BACK JOAN,' hung over the studio gate A red carpet was laid out leading to her dressing room, where she was welcomed with so many flowers from well wishers, two trestle tables had to be set up in the hall to accommodate them. It was a real life scene eerily similar to that of 'Norma Desmond's' comeback in the classic film, *Sunset Boulevard.*

Paramount Studios bought the script of *Lisbon* specifically for Joan, but without her prior script approval of their purchase, it was a costly mistake. Joan rejected the script simply because she wasn't about to play a character that loses her man to a younger woman. With the director, Irving Rapper standing firm and not wanting to alter the script to suit his potential leading lady, a stand off ensued and the project was reluctantly postponed. It was never made.

The western, *Johnny Guitar*, was a brave move, and according to Joan a moment of temporary insanity in deciding to star in it. In *Conversations with Joan Crawford*, Joan said, *"I should have had my head examined. No excuse for a picture being this bad or for me making it."*

The off screen fighting between Joan and her co-star, Mercedes McCambridge bordered on rivaling her legendary feuds with, Bette Davis. At one point, it got so bad, Joan stormed into the adjoining hotel room that McCambridge was using and threw all of her clothes out of the window and onto the highway below. Needless to say, McCambridge was moved to 'safer' housing the very next day. Like good films, bad films can equally achieve a level of cult status with the public - *Johnny Guitar* qualifies for the 'when bad films are good' category, even having it's own website, *The Johnny Guitar Appreciation Society.* A particularly interesting clause in Joan's, *Johnny Guitar,* contract is the so-called 'morality clause.' The following rules are listed under the title of 'conduct' - they read as follows:

You agree to conduct yourself with due regard to public conventions and morals. You also agree not to do or commit any act or thing that will degrade you or subject you to public hatred, contempt, scorn, ridicule or disrepute, or shock or offend the community or violate public morals or decency, or prejudice your standing in the community or us or the motion picture, theatrical, television, radio or entertainment industry in general, or that will tend to do any of the foregoing.

Joan lived her entire life by those rules of conduct. They didn't start and end with a film contract.

April 28, 1953 - Typed letter, to "Dore Freeman" of MGM Studios.

Dore dear -

My heart was so filled I could hardly speak - not only because of the beautiful red and white carnations, the magnificent cake for the "Torch Song Co", but the way you were there, comforting and assuring me at a time when I needed it so badly. You were just an angel - and are.

It was an unbelievably wonderful day for me, as you know - one I shall never forget. And yours - all your sweet thoughtfulness, coupled with the tangible expressions of your friendship - yours was a beautiful and enormous contribution to my memory. All right - I can say it in three words: "You're my hero!"

- Joan

April 30, 1953 - To "Mr and Mrs. R Roberts" of Long Island, N.Y.

Dear Sally and Bob -

Another year has passed for me and my life is richer, fuller and happier because of the thoughtfulness of my wonderful friends. Your card was so clever and did bring a broad smile to my face. To say 'Thank you' for remembering me is only a small way to tell you how much I deeply appreciated it.

My plans were changed somewhat and I have been at M.G.M. for the picture WHY SHOULD I CRY. It is not a complete musical, but a dramatic love story with music. I did enjoy rehearsing the dance routines although it meant many a long hour. We are now in production and will be finished in five weeks. I must be back at Paramount by June 1st for LISBON. This does keep me very busy from morning until night.

My own TV show has been delayed due to my crowded picture schedule. Also we are still in the negotiating stages. Do have a wonderful summer. May each day hold only happiness for each of you.

- Always - Joan

426 N. Bristol Ave.
Los Angeles 49, Calif.

June 6, 1953

My Dear Clifford Benson:

Thank you so much for your letter of June 2nd. Of
course I understand how busy you've been during the
Spring months and getting ready for all those visitors.
Thank you for wanting to name them after the children -
that is such a lovely thought and I hope your garden is
the most beautiful ever.

I'm so anxious to see the pictures you will take
with your Exakta VX. I obtained a copy of "Popular
Gardening" and saw the picture of the Joan Crawford iris.
The article was most informative and I'm delighted with
the beauty of "my namesake". Of course, I would love to
have whatever varieties you'd care to send and if the
"J.C." is your favorite, I will give it a choice spot.

We've just finished "Torch Song" at Metro - in
fact, we got our last shot today and I must say it's been
one of the most difficult - but fabulous and wonderful -
pictures I've ever made. You who love color so, will
adore the photography - I'm so anxious to have you see it.
I believe it should be coming your way no later than
October. We did the most difficult number - the "High
Yellow" - last and, believe me, there's very little left
of this tired "chorus girl" at the moment. But I think
we've made a really good picture and, after all, that's
what counts. The blisters on my feet will heal - the
back will stop aching - but I'll have made a good picture,
I hope.

I go right to Paramount for "Lisbon" after a couple
of days of fashion stills remaining to be shot at MGM.
So this coming week will be "moving" week for me. Then
getting settled at Paramount will be the next chore - but I'm
so happy to be busy I won't even mind not having a "day off".

I know your spring garden will be abundant and beautiful
and that you will have some outstanding creations this year.
Thank you for bringing me up to date in the midst of your
busy life..

God bless you.

JOAN CRAWFORD

Clifford Benson
1201 Verl Pl.
St. Louis 14, Mo.

June 4, 1953 - Typed letter, to "Dore Freeman" of MGM Studios. Referring to her role of "Jenny Stewart" in, *Torch Song*.

Dore Dear -
*   "How many petals on two dozen roses?" - About six thousand, I guess...and that's just about how many days we'll be friends. Don't count the days I'll be at Metro, honey - just count the days we'll know each other.*

*   What an angel, dream, sweetheart you were to send those, beautiful yellow roses, which lasted and lasted - another indication that we're here to stay -- you and I. Let's not think about when the picture is over -- it's been so wonderful that if I let myself think about leaving the lot - and you - and all the other wonderful people...well, I couldn't go on being Jenny Stewart. And I have to - for the next few days, anyway.*

*   Thank you, Dore, for what was just about the sweetest, most thoughtful gesture you could have made. And since I'm the sentimental type, too - well, they meant more than you could possibly know.*
*   Bless you - always....Joan.*

It was during the production of *Torch Song (1953)* that Joan and Elizabeth Taylor started a feud of their own. Elizabeth Taylor's second husband, Michael Wilding was Joan's co-star which meant that his wife was a frequent visitor on the set. It seems the war of words started after Elizabeth ignored one of Joan's early morning greetings. Furious, Joan went straight to publicity man, Dore Freeman and said, *"You tell that little bitch never to walk in here without acknowledging me! I want you to teach her some manners."*

Liz later retaliated, publicly, by telling reporters that her husband was very fortunate to be playing a blind man in his first American film. When asked why, she said, *"That way he doesn't have to look at Joan Crawford throughout the entire movie."*

June 6, 1953 - To 'Clifford Benson' of the 'American Iris Society.'

My Dear Clifford Benson:
*   Thank you so much for your letter of June 2nd. Of course I understand how busy you've been during the spring months and getting ready for all those visitors. Thank you for wanting to name them (the iris) after the children - that is such a lovely thought and I hope your garden is the most beautiful ever.*

*   I'm so anxious to see the pictures you will take with your Exacta VX. I obtained a copy of 'Popular Gardening' and saw the picture of the Joan Crawford iris. The article was most informative and I'm delighted*

with the beauty of 'my namesake'; Of course, I would love to have whatever varieties you'd care to send and if the 'J.C' is your favorite, I will give it a choice spot.

We've just finished 'Torch Song' at Metro - in fact, we got our last shot today and I must say it's been one of the most difficult - but fabulous and wonderful pictures I've ever made. You who love color so, will adore the photography - I'm so anxious to have you see it. I believe it should be coming your way no later than October. We did the most difficult number - the 'High Yellow' - last and, believe me, there's very little left of this tired 'chorus girl' at the moment. But I think we've made a really good picture and, after all, that's what counts. The blisters will heal - the back will stop aching - but I'll have made a good picture, I hope.

I go right to Paramount for 'Lisbon' after a couple of days of fashion stills remaining to be shot at MGM. So this coming week will be 'moving' week for me. Then getting settled at Paramount will be the next chore - but I'm so happy to be busy I won't even mind not having a 'day off.' I know your spring garden will be abundant and beautiful and that you will have some outstanding creations this year. Thank you for bringing me up to date in the midst of your busy life...

- God bless you - Joan Crawford.

April 13, 1953 - To Hollywood agent, 'H. N. Swanson.'

Dear Swanie,

Thank you so much for your letter of April 8th. M.C.A has already contacted me about this. At this time I do not want to do a series with Mildred Pierce - I would like to cut it down to an hour on a radio show transcribed, or a half hour for television, with M.C.A knows about. I just don't want to get into a female Dr. Christian at the moment. It's a good idea, but I just don't happen to want to get there yet. Give me another ten years before.... huh?

- Joan.

June 30, 1953 - Typed letter to "Dore Freeman" of MGM Studios.

Dore dear -

You know, you handed me a poem when I was leaving rather hurriedly one night and I put it away thinking I had put it with my mail. I either put it in my purse or in my pocket - and you know, I'm glad I did because I opened it today for the first time. I had tucked it from my pocket or my purse into my drawer and I opened it today because I probably needed it more today than I ever would have - and could enjoy it more. Not that I wouldn't have enjoyed it before, but it's one of the most beautiful, beautiful poems I've ever read.

And I'm not only proud of you for writing it - but I'm so deeply, deeply honored to have you give me a copy. There are no words - I wish I could write poetry like that - but since I can't there just are no words to tell you how grateful I am and how deeply I feel your friendship. You are, indeed, a wonderful, wonderful human being and how fortunate I am to have had a friend like you for so long. You've never faltered in your friendship or your loyalty or devotion. As a matter of fact, you're an even rarer human being than I thought because with the years, your devotion and loyalty grew stronger.

What can I ever do to repay you for that except to give you whatever friendship and loyalty and devotion I have - and my heart with all of its warmth extended in my hand to you. Bless you - and thank you again for the beautiful poem.

- Joan.

September 17, 1953 - Typed letter to, "Radie Harris" of The *Hollywood Reporter.*

Radie Dear,

I'm not going to talk about the party I gave for my Texas friends - not in a letter, or on a telephone. I'll speak to you about it when we next meet. There are so many personal things with your life - and my life - that we must talk to each other about. I, too, looked for that moment, but unfortunately, it didn't arrive.

I read your article today about Miss Dolores Gray. I remembered so well the night in Chasen's when you mentioned to Milton about, "Our girl's doing all right, isn't she?" No girl - or boy - is doing all right when she or he has failed to give the people who've helped them credit for a helping hand. Mary Martin is the most lovable, delightful, charming, gracious human being in the whole world - and I don't care who's name it is - if they do not help Mary Martin (I don't mean help because Mary Martin doesn't need that) - but if they aren't gracious enough to say, "I'm grateful - for Minnie Smith...Mary Martin.... whoever..." They don't deserve anything. You were so right about that. And some day (very soon) I hope I'll be able to tell you about the Texas party. God bless - I follow your column religiously. It's not only interesting, exciting because of the people you mention - it has a good healthy flavor about it - and this is rare, my girl.... real rare. Stick with it. Never you mind about what you're going to print - what will make real, topical, exciting reading.

You have a kind of quality, Radie that O.O. McIntyre had - strolling along Broadway. I couldn't give anyone a greater compliment.

Stick with it, please.... never mind about scandal, viciousness.... never you mind a bit. You'll outlast all of them. And until you find your pace and your stride, know that there are a great many of us who love you -

- Your devoted - Joan.

October 21, 1953 - Typed letter to, "Dore Freeman" of MGM Studios - From the set of, *Johnny Guitar.*

Dore Dear -

 This is just to say how much I miss you - way up here in Sedona, Arizona. And how I wish you were working on this picture. We not only have no publicity man - but no unit man...no nuthin'! - I don't know what's going to happen - but I sure wish you were here with us.

- My love as always - Joan.

October 26, 1953 - To 'Edith Lindeman' of the 'Richmond (Virginia) Times Dispatch –

In part...

Dear Edith,

 We're working terribly hard here on location. What with getting up at 3.30 AM for 7.00 AM shooting - work until 4.30 PM. Dinner is 5.30 PM (by the siren, and if you miss, you're out of luck!) Then we're working in story conference each night after shooting and by the time we adjourn - I'm ready to call it a day.... or really, a day and a half!

- Love, Joan.

October 29, 1953 - Typed letter to "Dore Freeman" of MGM Studios -

Dore Dear -

 What an angel you are...And you'd just better be interested in "our" premiere.... it just had to be good. I still wish you were here and how good you were to let me know you miss me and that life's dull.... I'm sorry life is dull - I could certainly improve that for you if I had you here.

 I wade in mountain streams - 28 degrees - fall off rocks -- and every time I come up for air I look for Dore. to help me. You'd have been right there with a blanket, some Mercurochrome for the skinned knees - just about anything else I need.

 Thank you for the picture, too. And I like my fanny and you were such an angel to replace it. This is something I mustn't lose...don't you agree?

- With love always - Joan.

November 14, 1953 - To reporter, W. Ward Marsh of the *Cleveland Plain Dealer* newspaper.

Ward Dear -
Someone not too long ago made a statement based, I assume on research, that more words have been written about me than any other actress in Hollywood and I'll go on the assumption that it's true. But in all my life and from the first word that was printed until now, I've never seen anything to compare with your article on November 1st. Ward, yours is the most beautifully written, kindest, most sympathetic, generous article I've ever read about me - or anybody else. And I think I'm not only the luckiest girl in the world to have inspired your remarks - but I'm the richest girl anywhere to have a friend like you.

Of course, the biographical portion is a faithful report of my career and the way you brought it up to and tied it in with 'Torch Song', makes me think that if and when my story is written, you and nobody but you should be allowed to do it. Your great understanding of my problems, the rapport, and sensitivity are all just unbelievable.

You say they should do a movie and title it, 'The Everlasting Glamour Girl', or 'The Eternal Female' or 'The Movie Queen.' Well, I just may write a book about you, Mr. W. Ward Marsh and call it, 'The Man Who Knows The True Human Being.' or just, 'The Greatest Guy I Know.' And you know something else? You've really challenged me this time. Now I want to be the actress and human being you've written about - to deserve a fraction of the wonderful things you said - to justify your belief in me and deserve your friendship. Now, I feel a little poem coming on. Would you mind Ward if I say it this way: "All that you think and believe about me. These are the things I'm trying to be." ...all right, so it's not a very long poem, but it's straight from the heart of your devoted...
- Joan Crawford.

November 18, 1953 - To 'Nate Perlstein' of 'Pabst Brewery,' Los Angeles, California.

My Dear Nate Perlstein,
I just adored my scroll announcing your party for the opening of the new Pabst Brewery - and my mug which I shall use to great advantage in my dressing room at Republic where I am now staying during the making of my western film. How I wish I could be with you on the 24th - but I have a late call that day and we'll shoot some night scenes, so I'm sure I could never make it. Thank you so much for wanting me to be with you on this occasion. I'm deeply grateful for the invitation and gift.
- Joan Crawford.

December 8, 1953 - To, 'Sally Roberts' on 426 North Bristol Avenue, letterhead.

Sally Dear,

Thank you so much for telling me you saw and liked, 'Torch Song' - you said wonderful things about both the picture and me - I'll work very hard to try to deserve them. I was just on the last few days of my western, 'Johnny Guitar', when the flu bug hit me in addition to an attack of pleurisy and I'm at home today. I expect to be back to work tomorrow, however, and finish the picture. Next come the holidays with the flurry and excitement of Christmas and the four children at home.

Thank you for saying you'd like to meet me. I'm sure we will have that mutual pleasure some day, Sally. Do let me know if you plan a trip out this way, so I can plan to have time for a visit. . And again, thank you for being such a dear, loyal friend to your deeply grateful.

- Joan Crawford.

April 14, 1954 - Typed letter to, "William Thomas" of Paramount Studios.

Bill darling -

Thank you so much for your charming wire on my birthday. Life has been very full and hectic, what with scripts, children needing doctors, dentists, eye doctors, etc, etc. And now I'm off to a ranch with all four children on their Easter vacation.

Thank you for our conversation yesterday...I received the script today and will get at it real quick. God bless.... thank you, darling.... and a Happy Easter to you is the wish of...Joan.

May 26, 1954 - To 'Mrs. Charles S. Barnett,' Wheeling, West Virginia.

Dear Lila,

Please do not think me ungrateful for the lovely greeting card you sent to me. I was away for my birthday and again at Easter and have been working day and night since I returned to catch up. Thank you again and again for your ever thoughtfulness of me.

I am rushing like mad as I am leaving on a two-week tour of Texas to help open my western picture. I am going to Dallas, Fort Worth, Houston and San Antonio. I am so excited over the press conferences, the making of tape recordings and the many luncheons we have planned. I know it will give me an opportunity to meet so many new friends. It is a hectic schedule for so short a time, but I know I will enjoy every minute I am gone.

My plans for TV will be held up until I return. I do have several sponsors who are interested and it is just a matter of finding the right time. I still haven't any definite plans for my next picture. Again, let me say how much I have enjoyed your dear, loyal friendship. Best of wishes to you and yours for a summer of much happiness.

- Sincerely yours, Joan Crawford.

June 24, 1954 - To Cynthia and Susan Miles, two little girls from Illinois, USA.

Dear Cynthia and Susan -

How delighted I was, Cynthia and Susan, to find your sweet birthday card and the darling handkerchief with the cute poodle in the corner. To know you picked it out yourself made me love it all the more. Thank you both from the bottom of my heart.

You were surely good little girls to sit through "Torch Song" three times without even a single wiggle, as your mommy says. I am glad you like to dance for it is lots of fun.

Cathy was so disappointed she couldn't go back to school for the closing days. Her arm is coming along just fine and we are so happy she didn't have to miss a lot of school. We are all looking forward to the summer.

Both of you girls have a happy summer with lots of fun each day. Again, many, many thanks for remembering me in such a sweet way.

- Sincerely Joan Crawford.

September 9, 1954 - Typed letter to "Dore Freeman" of MGM Studios.

Dore, darling -

Thank you for your letter of Wednesday, midnight. You know I know that you're always there.... You just got my letter telling you that. Thank you, too, for giving me whatever, "C. Crawford's" first name turns out to be. How sweet you were to bring the birds, food and sand over. I'd like so much to pay for everything...Please let me. You just can't keep on giving all your life. Thank you, my darling, for everything.

I'm sorry dinner was so slow. I'm sorry I wasn't glamorous and beautiful and all done up. I'm a working gal and, as I said, I just can't get over being 'Mildred Pierce.' Please send the bill. You know I won't be happy any other way. God bless.

- My love, always - Joan.

January 16th, 1955 - To 'Mrs. Charles S. Barnett' Wheeling, West Virginia.

Dear Lila,

Thank you so much for remembering us at Christmas time with your lovely greeting. The children were home during vacation and so excited. Our holidays were delightful and we're very grateful to everyone.

I'm still in production at Universal-International and love it here. It's wonderful making a picture again. May the New Year bring you everything your heart desires is the wish of...

- Joan Crawford.

July 1st, 1955.

Dear Sally and Bob,

What a dear you are. Thank you from the bottom of my grateful heart for your sweet note wishing me happiness. Our European trip was delightful and so restful. Everyone was wonderful...I'm sure I'll never forget them. I just couldn't be happier and only wish everyone in the world could be as happy as I am now, and know I always will be. I'm so busy again as production will soon start on 'The Way We Are' at Columbia. Again, thank you for your sweet thoughtfulness.

- Gratefully, Joan Crawford.

October 25, 1955 - A particularly lengthy nine-page letter, answering questions put to her about her career.

Dear Larry,

Thank you so much for your sweet letter and here we go with the answers to your questions. Incidentally, before I start, my itinerary is Chicago, October 30, 31 and November 1, St. Louis November 2 and 3, New Orleans November 5 and 6, Jacksonville November 7 and 8, Miami Beach November 9 through 16, Detroit November 18, finish in Salt Lake City and return to Los Angeles November 3. It doesn't look as if Boston will be on it, but just know, that if I do get there, you'll be the first one I see.

1) Do I have a complete list of my films? No, I don't, but if you write to Dore Freeman, in care of MGM Publicity, Culver City, California and ask him, he'll see that you get it immediately.

2) About Mr. Thalberg. Larry, Mr. Thalberg had very little to do with my career. I only came in contact with Mr. Thalberg a couple of times and then only briefly.

3) Why did I leave Warners to engage in independent free-lance work? Because I felt Warners was putting me in mediocre things. After important material like, 'Mildred Pierce,' 'Humoresque,' 'Possessed,' I suddenly got into a rut of very mediocre films and then asked for my release.

4) Has every picture since 'Sudden Fear' been done by me on a profit percentage basis? - Were any of your films prior to 1952 done under that arrangement? - No 'Sudden Fear' was the first, 'Johnny Guitar' I got straight salary for, as I did on 'Female on the Beach.'
'Queen Bee' and 'The Way We Are' are my productions, percentage wise.

5) About costumes pictures. Larry, I'm sending your questions back to you so you will be able to read them so we don't have to retype them, okay? I think the reason I have played so few costume pictures is the fact that everyone at Metro thought me so typically modern. I have no personal aversion to them. I'm just interested in good pictures, regardless of the era.

6) No, December 1926 was when I actually signed my first deal with MGM.

7) When I worked with Mr. Gilbert (John Gilbert), he was so desperately and deeply and frantically in love with Miss Garbo (Greta Garbo), that it was hard for him to concentrate on his work. We all tried to be as patient and thoughtful as we could. I learned a great deal from him and Lon Chaney and from everyone I've worked with.

8) I have only the highest, highest praise for Miss Garbo and Miss Shearer. I've worked with Miss Shearer a couple of times, Garbo in 'Grand Hotel,' but never had any scenes with her. How I wish she'd come back to pictures. There is only one Miss Garbo, such talent, such beauty. What a shame it is not being put to use in this wonderful medium of ours.

9) Thank you for saying, 'Possessed' is most frequently spoken of as the best acting performance, I have turned in. I felt it was too. As a matter of fact, just before we started 'The Way We Are,' I ran the picture for Cliff Robertson, who has to play a schizophrenic in that picture. I still think 'Possessed' is one of my better pictures. I think you will agree that "Queen Bee" and 'The Way We Are' will be in that category. I hope you will, at least, because that's my opinion.

10) The story of 'Lisbon' was originally written for Mr. William Holden. It's a man's story, never could, even though they tried, be transposed into a woman's story. That's why I never did it. Paramount was simply magnificent about it.

11) I have no TV plans. As you know, I have just completed 'The Way We Are' last night, and I'm headed on tour Friday for 'Queen Bee.' After that I spend Thanksgiving and Christmas here with the children, and then I go to Europe to make 'The Story of Esther Costello' in the spring.

12) No, I do not have a 'Memento Room.' I have photographs of a lot of people, but they are in books and in a closet. I do have a collection of eight by ten stills from each film, neatly bound in navy blue leather with the title of the picture on the cover in gold. I do not believe in 'Memento Rooms,' at least for the home I want to live in. I believe that my life is reflected in my being and I want only the good things to be reflected for my family and for my friends. Most of my press clippings were thrown out to make room for all the children and their cribs and bassinets and bottles, etc., but many, many times, friends and fans who have collected clippings over the years have seen to it that I have gotten their scrap books, so that I have them for the children, in case they are interested.

13) Indeed I was shopping carefully. The longer you are in pictures, the more carefully you have to shop.

14) Yes, I did fight against doing 'Flamingo Road' until they rewrote the script. 'Harriet Craig' was certainly not a choice of mine. 'Goodbye My Fancy' could have been a much more interesting picture, but unfortunately it had a political angle in it which was cut out, which also took the guts out of it.

15) My personal and professional estimate of Margaret Sullivan is 500 per cent. I think she is a great, great lady and a very, fine artist and I adore her personally. I think the picture was underestimated, 'The Shining Hour.'

I think it had a brilliant cast with Margaret Sullivan, Fay Bainter, Bob Young, Melvyn Douglas and of course, Mr. Mankiewisz writing it and producing it. I don't know when I was happier professionally than when I made that picture.

16) On a 'Woman's Face' I ran the Swedish version with Ingrid Bergman in it and begged Mr. Mayer to buy it, which he did, so we made the American version with Mr. George Cukor, and that was a very, very happy period of my life. 'Susan and God' was my choice, yes. I think your list is just sensational. That would be my choice too, with the exception of the last two, 'Queen Bee' and 'The Way We Are.' Please let me know what you think of the latter two, when you do see them. Bless you?

17) No, I didn't feel any artistic frustration during the 'clothes-horse' period.

18) I thought 'Ice Follies' was a very mediocre film, but after all, when you are under contract, you do what the studio tells you. Perhaps that's why I like being free, so I can do what I choose.

19) Yes, 'Untamed' in 1929 was the first time my voice was heard. I had never studied voice or with a vocal coach when I did "Untamed". I did, however, afterwards study six years for opera, but nothing came of it. You ask me about 'my fine carriage', posture, walk, etc.'

It is something I work on each day, even when I'm doing housework. I try to walk straight and erect.

20) I see Mary Pickford quite frequently at social functions. We are very close, very friendly and very warm.

21) I have no idea how many times I have redecorated the house. Mr. Haines has done it a couple of times. I do plan to sell it and build a more practical house, particularly now that the children are growing up.

22) I want my children to have a happy and full life, and if acting is part of it, then I want them to have that. My oldest daughter, Christina, is very anxious to study drama, but only for theater. She has no desire for pictures. I doubt very much if Christopher will be in the acting profession, and the babies are a little too young to tell.

23) Have I made out a master plan for my career over the next ten years or so? - No, not that far in advance. No, to your question, will I ever want to retire. No, never. Yes, I did consider the play opposite Charles Boyer, "Kind Sir', and I decided against it, because I was just frightened. I felt that my career was in pictures and that I wasn't ready to tackle a new medium yet.

24) Yes, I would like very much to try a play. But first I would like to go to work for about three summers in summer stock and play small parts, help with the production, help with the direction and be part of it. Then perhaps I would have more courage to go on and do the starring part.

25) The man who has helped me most in my career is L.B. Mayer. There have been many other people who have helped, but he has been the most consistent helper and at a time when I needed help during formative years.

Now, as to the list of my films and release dates, please write to Dore Freeman, as I suggested before. God bless. I hope I have done a fairly good job for you. Any other questions or any one you want elongated, just send me more and I will get them when I return from tour.

- Goodbye for now, Joan.

November 26, 1955. - A newsy thank you note on the occasion of her marriage to Pepsi-Cola boss, Al Steele.

Dear Bertie and Peete,

Thank you for your beautiful card, and for your sweet letter. I am so deeply grateful to you for your good wishes and kind thoughts about my marriage. I just couldn't be happier and I know I always will be.

The past month, I have been on tour for 'Queen Bee'. I had a delightful time.... Everyone was so enthusiastic. I loved the South, and it was a real pleasure meeting those wonderful Southern people. Their

426 NORTH BRISTOL AVENUE
LOS ANGELES 49, CALIFORNIA

January 31, 1956

Dear Roy Schooler,

Thank you not only for your
lovely Christmas card but for your
sweet letter and your snapshot. I
am so deeply grateful to you for
remembering me.

I am delighted you have seen
all of my pictures and associate
them with some event in your life.
Bless you for telling me.

Our holiday in Europe was
perfect. Switzerland is an enchanting country. How the children loved the snow. They had a
wonderful time, and my husband
and I got a much needed rest.
Before returning home, we had
an enjoyable tour of France.

Thank you again and may the
New Year bring you all that is
good is the wish of

JOAN CRAWFORD

hospitality and friendliness overwhelmed me. Our Thanksgiving was lovely. With Christmas nearing, we are busy making plans for the holidays. Again thank you and God bless each of you for your sweet thoughtfulness.

- Gratefully, Joan Crawford.

January 31st, 1956.

My Darling Pearlina,
How sweet you were to send that lovely Christmas card to us. As you know, we are just rushed to pieces, so I hope you will forgive me for being so late in thanking you. We had the most heavenly time in Switzerland, and the children were enchanted wit St. Moritz in the snow. It was a veritable fairyland. It was the happiest Christmas that we can ever remember. May 1956 bring you much happiness is the wish of a grateful.

- Joan Crawford.

March 24, 1956 - On '426 North Bristol Avenue' letterhead ~

Dear Bertie and Pete,
Your delightful letter and sweet birthday card were waiting for me upon my arrival home this week. Thank you from the bottom of my heart for remembering me. Being able to spend my special day with my family completed my happiness.
My husband and I have just returned from a delightful vacation in Jamaica. What an enchanting and beautiful country. We loved Montego Bay. Yes, I am completing plans for my next picture. I am going to England, Ireland and Scotland to make, 'The Story of Esther Costello'. Production will start the early part of this summer.
Again thank you for your sweet thoughtfulness. God bless each of you. May you have a Joyous Easter is the wish of a grateful...

- Joan Crawford.

May 31, 1956 - This letter and the following letter were written on the same day, notice she mentions the similar things, but still, she phrases them differently for each letter.

Dear Sally and Bob -
Thank you so much for your charming letter of April 3rd. I am sorry I haven't answered before this, but I have been commuting between New York and Los Angeles, by train, and I've had difficulty keeping up with my correspondence.

119

My husband and I have bought a new apartment in New York.
William Haines' men are doing extensive remodeling and redecorating for
us. We will not be able to move in until December.

I am rushing like mad as I am having fittings for thirty-eight
costumes for 'The Story of Esther Costello.' I'll be leaving for England in
July, and production will start there in August. Rossano Brazzi will play
my husband. It is being filmed by a British crew.

I hope I can meet both of you. My trips to New York have been
such quick ones, and I do spend every minute I can with my husband. Do
let me hear from you again. Your mail will be forwarded to me in England.
Best wishes, always, Gratefully

- Joan.

May 31, 1956 - On '426 North Bristol Avenue' letterhead ~

Dear Bertie and Pete,
Thank you so much for the beautiful wedding anniversary card.
We deeply appreciate your sweet thoughtfulness. Thank you, too, for the
lovely Mother's Day card and for your sweet letters. You are such dear
thoughtful friends. God bless you...

Our new apartment is progressing nicely. We are having it
remodeled and redecorated and it will be ready for us in December. I am
so busy having thirty-eight costumes fitted for the 'Story of Esther
Costello'. I leave for England in July, and production will start there in
August. Again thank you...and we send our very best wishes to you -

- Gratefully, Joan Crawford.

July 11, 1956.

Dear Bertie and Pete,
Thank you so much for your delightful letter of July 2nd - I am
rushing like mad having fittings during the daytime (at the studio), story
conferences in the evening, and then spending half the night doing my
personal packing. I love it all.

I leave for New York on Thursday and my husband and I will sail
on July 19th for England, 'The Story of Esther Costello', goes into
production on August 18th at the Shepperton Studios, just outside of
London. We will have some location work in Ireland and Scotland, but
most of the film will be made in England. I am so excited, I can hardly
wait.

The children are in summer camp now. Cynthia and Cathy and
their governess will fly to London to spend the month of August with me.
How wonderful you have been promoted to Service Manager at the

120

Typewriter Exchange - Congratulations Pete! Again, thank you for your lovely letter. Bless you...and I send my very best wishes to you.

- Gratefully, Joan Crawford.

August 30, 1956. - Having just started work on 'The Story of Esther Costello.'

Dear Bertie and Peete,

Thank you so much for your lovely card and for your sweet letter. I am in England now and production has started on my picture. We are working such long hours, but I love every minute of it. I am looking forward to going to Scotland and Ireland for some of the filming. We have an entire British crew, and I do enjoy working with them.

The twins and their governess have been with me since August 2nd. They love it here, but will soon be leaving so they can get home for the start of school in September. I do like England...The beautiful countryside is so peaceful...And the people are very charming. I know my stay of five months will be pleasant.

Forgive the brevity of this, but I am due at the studio. I am sending your letter, with others, to my house in California, and it will be mailed from there. Do write again, as my mail is forwarded to me. My best wishes to each of you.

- Gratefully, J.C.

October 16, 1956.

Dear Bob Jean,

Your lovely letter and your cards have just reached me. I enjoy hearing from you so much. Thank you for writing. I am delighted that you enjoyed 'Autumn Leaves' so much that you saw it several times. We enjoyed making it. Yes, I too, think Cliff Robertson did a wonderful job. He is a very charming person, and a brilliant actor. I am deeply grateful for all the nice things you had to say.

'The Story of Esther Costello' is progressing nicely. Yes, Rossano Brazzi, plays my husband. Heather Sears, plays 'Esther' and John Loder is also in the cast. Our plans were changed and we did not go to Ireland on location. A very realistic set was made here, at the studios, and we shot all the necessary scenes from it. We are working such long hours as we want to complete the film by December 15th. I probably will not be home until after the first of the year.

Thank you again for writing...And thank you for your enthusiastic praise for 'Autumn Leaves.' Bless you...

- Gratefully, J.C.

Autumn Leaves, was Joan's first film after her marriage to Alfred Steele, her happy marriage and the positive reviews of the film must have contributed to one of the most satisfying moments of her life. Finally, both her personal and professional lives had blended successfully.

Robert Aldrich, directed the film, later teaming up with Joan once more as he took the directors chair in, *Whatever Happened to Baby Jane? (1962)*, also starring Bette Davis.

Marjorie Bennett, plays the waitress in the diner (*Autumn Leaves*) where Millicent (Joan) and Burt (Cliff Robertson) first meet. Seven years later we see her play Victor Buono's mother in, *Whatever Happened To Baby Jane? (1962)*.

November 28, 1956.

Dear Bertie and Pete,

Your delightful letter of November 15th was forwarded to me here in England. Thank you so much for writing, I am very happy that you enjoyed, 'Autumn Leaves.' Yes, Cliff Robertson is a wonderful person, and a very brilliant actor. I am glad you liked him.

We are getting along nicely with the film, 'The Story of Esther Costello' - I think we are going to have a picture we can all be proud of, and one that should do a great deal of good for blind people all over the world.

My presentation to the Queen was very exciting. I was terribly nervous but the Queen and Princess Margaret put me at ease immediately. They are so lovely and gracious.

I do not know where we will spend the holidays. If I do not finish the film by December 12th, so I can catch the last boat to the United States, then we will probably go to Switzerland for Christmas. The children will join us, wherever we are. Since it is getting toward the Christmas Season, I would like to take this opportunity to wish each of you the merriest of holidays, and may the New Year bring you happiness and prosperity.

- Gratefully, Joan Crawford.

Joan was co- producer on the film and her sharp business sense saw her cut the initial $70,000 budget down to $40,000. Her flat $200,000 salary was boosted by giving her a ten percent cut of the films profits. It was a thank you from the American Film Corporation for going above and beyond the terms of her contract.

January 17, 1957 -

Dear Bertie and Pete,

Thank you so very much for your beautiful, beautiful Christmas card. You are such dears and always so thoughtful. Bless you. We spent the holidays in Switzerland and had such a delightful time. Just before Christmas, the children and our poodles flew over and joined us. You should see this heavenly country...It's just like a fairyland. The children loved the snow and had the time of their lives skiing and skating.

I do hope you had a wonderful Christmas and may the New Year being you everything you wish for yourselves -

- Gratefully - Joan Crawford.

March 13, 1957.

Arthur dear,

Enclosed is part of the itinerary for the immediate future. Will write later. I think it is wise that Kurt Bernhardt wait until further developments. Alfred is in the New York Hospital, and will be there for about ten days, so whenever you wish to talk to me, wire me at 36 Sutton Place and I will call you from the hospital.

- Love, Joan.

A decade prior to this letter being written, Kurt Bernhardt directed Joan in her Oscar nominated role, *Possessed*. Up until and beyond the years of this letter being written, they failed to collaborate on another project together. The 1947 release of *Possessed* was to be their only professional encounter. Still, after reading the second paragraph of the above letter, it's obvious another attempt at 'something' was being arranged. It never happened.

April 1, 1957 - On 'J.C' personal letterhead to 'Bob Jean.'

Dear Bob,

Thank you so much for remembering my birthday with your lovely card. I also want to thank you for your delightful letters. I have been rushing like mad getting ready to leave with my husband on our tour of the South for Pepsi-Cola. We plan to be gone two months and hope to spend Easter in Bermuda. We will take Cathy and Cynthia with us, if they are over the measles by then. I do hope you will have a joyous Easter. Bless you and my warmest wishes to you.

- Gratefully, J.C.

April 9, 1957 - On '426 North Bristol Avenue' letterhead.

Dear Bertie and Pete,

Thank you so much for your delightful letter and for your beautiful birthday card. My birthday was March 23rd. I did spend a very quiet but happy day with my husband. We expect to be doing a great deal of traveling during the next two months. We are going on a Pepsi-Cola tour of the United States and after that, it is entirely possible we will go to Bermuda for a short holiday.

We have not moved into our new apartment as yet. It will be several months before it will be completed. They are so slow. The children are fine. They are looking forward to Easter...Cathy and Cynthia hope to be over the measles by then. Again, thank you for remembering me. My warmest wishes to both of you for a Joyous Easter.

- Bless you...Gratefully, Joan.

August 26, 1957 -

May dear,

Your wonderful letter of August 16th was forwarded to me, and I am so delighted that you loved, 'The Story of Esther Costello'. Your letter is the first one I've received from England since the picture was released there, and God bless you for seeing it the first day, and for giving me so much first-hand information about its opening there. Thank you so much, too, May, for sending me all these clippings. Needless to say, the reviews make me very happy.

And your comments on the picture are brilliant and complimentary, May. I'm so pleased that the picture brought you such enjoyment. And bless you for telling me about it so promptly. My husband and I are on a business trip in the Middle East and South Africa. We are having a fabulously exciting tour. The heat is pretty grim, but bearable because of my beloved Alfred. The people are very friendly, and embrace me as if I were a part of them.

We'll return to California next month, to put the twins in school. They are spending the summer at our home in Los Angeles, and I'm dying to see them again - I miss them so.

- Joan.

February 21, 1958 - Typed letter to 'Bill Frye' on "Joan Crawford" imprinted stationary.

Bill dear,

How can I ever thank you for all the help you have given us on this film: it is such a joy to work with you, and you have wonderfully brilliant and original ideas and plans to improve the film. The white lilacs and tulips are just enchanting and beautiful beyond belief. Thank you so much for being so thoughtful, and for helping to make these days so pleasant for me. God bless, and I do hope that we will have occasion to work together often in the future.

- Joan.

This letter is particularly amusing because one of Joan's false eyelashes was stuck to the paper. After all these years, it still is, however it had to have been an accident, since she makes no mention of sending the eyelash within the content of the letter itself.

February 22, 1958 - To "Sally Roberts" of Forest Hills, N.Y.

Dear Sally,

Thank you for your good letter. I shall be happy to have a Pepsi - Cola lighter sent to you, and I hope you'll enjoy playing the little Pepsi-Cola jingle. It's sweet of you to ask for one, for your collection.

My husband, the children and I had a wonderful three weeks vacation in Acapulco and Mexico City, and returned on the 12th. I've been spending all of this week filming a General Electric Theatre television show, which will be shown Sunday Night, March 23rd. I hope you'll be able to see it. Bless you and thank you again for writing.

- Joan.

April 3, 1958 - To 'Sally and Bob Roberts' - Long Island, N.Y.

Dear Sally and Bob,

Thank you so much for the charming card you sent for my birthday, and for all your good wishes. It was very sweet of you to remember the day, and I can't tell you how much your thoughtfulness meant to me.

I am so pleased; Sally, that you received the little music box Pepsi-Cola lighter, and that you are enjoying it, and have added it to your music box collection. Bless you and a very happy Easter to you.

- Joan.

August 29, 1958 - To gossip columnist - 'Hedda Hopper.'

Hedda darling,
Thank you so much for your beautiful expressions of sympathy. It was so sweet of you to send the lovely large spray of gladioli, stock and roses to Mother's funeral. We are so deeply grateful to you. The flowers were exquisite. I know Mother would have adored them.
She looked so beautiful. I placed her in the private gardens at Forest Lawn, in the sun, surrounded by the lovely flowers and shrubbery which she loved so much.

- Love, Joan.

September 12, 1958.

Dear Bertie,
Thank you so much for your sweet letter and lovely card. I enjoyed hearing from you again. Our tour of Europe was lovely. We visited Brussels and the World's Fair there, then through Holland, and Copenhagen, Denmark, and to Hamburg, Germany, and Dusseldorf; took a boat and stayed at a beautiful, old castle near Frankfurt for a week. Then we spent a few days in Paris, and came home by boat, on the "United States."
We found many of the cities so enchanting and quaint. I particularly loved Hamburg and Copenhagen, and they were like stepping into a land of folklore. Do write again.........Until then, I send my best wishes to you and your husband.

- As always, Joan Crawford.

December 1st, 1958. - To 'Robert Feltch' of Hanover, Pa.

Dear Robert,
How nice to hear from you again. Thank you so much for your charming letter. We have just spent a week in Atlantic City, attending a convention, and had a delightful time. It's an exciting city, and my first visit. We wished the children could have been with us, but - alas - they were in school.
I hope you will enjoy watching the General Electric Theater show we have filmed. The title is 'And One Was Loyal' and Tom Holmore ad Robert Douglas are in the cast with me. It will be shown on television on January 4th in most cities, I understand. Every good wish to you, and I do hope you had a happy Thanksgiving.

- As always, J.C.

May 9, 1959 - Typed letter on "Mrs. Alfred Nu Steele" imprinted stationary.

My dear Mr. Walders,
Thank you so much for giving Mr. Cox the tape that my husband and I did. I'm so glad I asked for it. How gracious you were to give it to me. After the tragedy, there's all the more reason why I'd want to keep it. Bless you, and thank you for being so very kind and gracious to
- Joan Crawford.

May 9, 1959 - On 'Mrs. Alfred N. Steele' Stationery.

Herb dear,
Thank you so much for your dear sweet message. It means more to me than you'll ever know. I'm deeply grateful and I know Alfred would be grateful too for the comfort that your friendship brings me in my time of need. Your beautiful thoughts, as only you can put them into words, will give me great comfort.
Bless you and I hope to see you soon.
- Love Joan

P.S - (Handwritten post script) - *So happy you are in town - got your message today about the Museum of Modern Art Film Library - I leave Wednesday - but I've just got to find time tomorrow to say hello.*

On April 19th, 1959, Joan's fourth and last husband dies in his sleep. This *"thank you for your sympathy"* letter was one of thousands of responses that were sent out by Joan showing her appreciation of friends and fans condolence cards and letters that flooded her New York apartment in the weeks following Alfred Steele's death. She was a widow for the very first time, but her grief didn't stop her from continuing what her husband had left behind. Just a few weeks after his death, by May of 1959, she would replace her husband on the board of the Pepsi Cola Company.

In a letter to me, the author of this book, the Senior Consumer Representative of Pepsi Cola Company, Rebecca L. Smith, writes of Pepsi's continued memories of Joan Crawford: January 7th, 2003. - In part - *"...Miss Crawford was a very well loved member of the Pepsi family and remains fondly in the hearts of many of us here today. In 1955, Miss Crawford married former Pepsi President, Al Steele. And for several years, Miss Crawford traveled with her husband promoting Pepsi all over the world. Even after her husband's death, in 1959, Miss Crawford continued her affiliation with Pepsi and served as a member of the board and as a good-will ambassador until 1974.........."*

May 31, 1959 - To columnist 'Jack Gabriel' at NEA Service in New York.

Dear Jack,
     Thank you so much for all the wonderful things you had to say to me. I do miss him (Al Steele) so terribly. There are times when I feel like an empty shell that aches. I'm now making a film. One day maybe I'll do 'Lucy Crown.' I'm only doing four scenes in this picture at 20th. God bless
                                                         - Joan.

September 8th, 1959 - An unusually scathing letter to a 'Walter B. Smalley' of Washington D.C.

My dear Walter,
     Thank you for your dear, sweet letter of September 3rd. I have never been 'noisy' in my life. I have too much respect for talent. The article you read said that I was late, not 'noisy.' I was late because we went through a very bad storm driving to Washington to get to the opening of 'Heartbreak House'. I read every review and interview in Washington, and no one said I was 'noisy' --- at least not in print. They couldn't very well, since it's not true.
     I am not working for Mr. Rose, nor do I propose to do a musical or any other play. I was merely his guest. I wish you great success in your writing -- whether it be under your name or a pen name. Please do not believe everything you hear or read and be a good accurate writer and check the source from whence it comes. You say I'm a 'very capable woman.' Yes, but I am also a professional woman and I have too much respect for professional people and artists to be 'noisy' during a performance.
                                         - Bless you, Joan Crawford.

October 12, 1959 - To 'Shirley Eder' of the *Detroit Free Press*, Detroit, Michigan.

Shirley Dear,
     Now you just put down the white carpets and you just make everybody take their shoes off right at the elevator - period!! - Live luxuriously...Live beautifully...Live dangerously...And, tell your friends if they don't want to take their shoes off, they can't come to your house. It's that simple. Bye for now. Let me know when you're in New York next.
                                              - Love, Joan.

The Letters...1960's

Jane - (Bette Davis) to Blanche (Joan) -

"All right Blanche, miss big fat movie star, miss rotten stinking actress, press a button, ring a bell and you think the whole world comes running!"

- Whatever Happened to Baby Jane? (1962).

There's a great deal of correspondence during this decade (and to a lesser degree into the 1970's) between Joan and one of her good friends, Mrs. Frances Spingold. Nate B. and Frances Spingold were a very wealthy New York couple who devoted most of their lives to the arts.

Joan became meshed into their world when Nate became an active member of the "William Morris Agency." Their impressive client list stretched from film to theater. Nate eventually moved on to become the executive vice-president of Columbia Pictures and played an integral part in developing the motion picture as we know it today.

After an early marriage that ended in divorce, Frances married Nate in 1911. She was widowed in 1958, after 47 years of marriage. The Spingold's were thought to have owned the most impressive, most valuable private art collection in the United States. Their homes were virtual art museums, consisting of such diverse works as French Impressionists thru to modern artists. The Museum of Modern Art, in New York City, now houses many of the paintings from their multi million-dollar estate collection.

A year before Nate's death, the couple visited Brandeis College and were so impressed with their dedication to the arts that Nate willed a major portion of his estate to the University. That bequest was for millions of dollars, and they put it to good use, building the impressive theater arts center in their name. The "Spingold Theater" was completed and opened in 1965.

Joan accepting Anne Bancroft's Oscar at the 35th Academy Awards ceremony in 1962.

The "Joan Crawford School of Dance" is another Brandeis University program, which was no doubt one of Frances' suggestions. The school displays many of Joan's awards given to her throughout her career, and to this day, provides an in depth study of the art of dance for those students wanting to pursue a career in the field.

Frances' dedication to Joan is extraordinary. At the time of their most frequent correspondence, Frances was widowed, elderly, not of good health and spending her "golden years" between her luxury homes in New York and Palm Springs. She seemed to crave the next letter from Joan, almost begging her in some of them to write as soon as she can. Joan didn't disappoint, as you will see, their letters are gossipy and full of information

May 19, 1960 -

Dear Bertie and Pete,

Thank you so much for sending me the beautiful Easter card and for your sweet letter. How kind and thoughtful you always are, and I am deeply grateful.

I have just returned for Las Vegas, where I attended a dedication for my late husband, and then I went to Modesto, Santa Rosa and San Francisco on business for Pepsi-Cola. God Bless, and my best wishes always.

- Joan.

September 15, 1960 - 8:48 AM - Western Union Telegram to 'Ross Hunter.'

Ross Dear,

I tried to reach you for five days. That character has my name on it. Pin it down boy. I'm not about to let go of it.

- Love, Joan Crawford.

Approximately one month after the above letter was written, in October of 1960, Joan's eldest daughter, Christina releases a statement saying that she and her mother are on opposite sides of a *"deep chasm of misunderstanding."* Joan later reiterated her words by saying, *"It's been eighteen years of disappointment."*

The year got worse for Joan when on November 15, 1960, she got word that her costar and on again, off again lover, Clark Gable had succumbed to a heart attack. She was so grief stricken by the news that she was unable to release a statement to the media.

131

February 5, 1961 - To a friend who needs some diet advice.

My dear Jim,

Thank you so much for your very nice letter of the 26th. It was a joy to hear from you again. How nice that you saw the twins and me on 'What's my line?' - I'm so pleased you enjoyed the show. Now, why don't you try doing something - why don't you try eating, in the morning, two eggs, soft boiled, four pieces of bacon, and if you drink coffee, only one cup, without cream or sugar, and one half grapefruit.

For lunch, have one small steak or two single lamb chops, spinach, either cooked or raw, one cup of coffee or tea, without cream or sugar, and one half grapefruit.

For dinner, if you have had steak for lunch, then eat two single lamb chops. But if you did have the lamb chops for lunch, than have steak for dinner. You might prefer chicken. But don't eat dumplings, spaghetti or potatoes. Have spinach or carrots or another green vegetable, and one half grapefruit. Don't eat bread, butter or desserts, and leave the table hungry. Don't eat in between meals either. Try it for two months and see what happens. Just try it for me, would you please. It's going to be tough for the first week. After that, I don't think you'll mind it.

I have signed for a television series. I don't know when we are going to work on it yet. The scripts are being prepared now. It takes a long time to get all the business arrangements ironed out. Thank you again for the lovely oranges, but mostly for your fine friendship.

- Joan Crawford.

February 14, 1961.

Dear Rosalie,

Thank you for your sweet letter, sent to New York, which was just forwarded to me. I am so pleased that you enjoyed the Zane Grey Theatre show. I know you must miss Ken. The six months will go fast, if you keep busy, I know. I am so sad to hear about your friend, James Mulligan. I am sending an autographed photograph to him today. Do let me know how he is coming along. Incidentally, I would suggest that you use my Hollywood address, as when I am traveling, my mail in New York is not forwarded promptly. However, the mail in Hollywood reaches me wherever I am.

- All good wishes to you – Joan.

In August of 1961, Joan is a special guest judge on the Miss America Pageant.

October 13, 1961.

Dear Cecil,

Thank you for your good air letters, and for all the news of your travels. You must have had a divine motor trip to Denmark, Sweden and Germany. It sounds so interesting.

I have been doing a bit of television work lately, and will be on a panel show, "I've Got a Secret", on October 23, and another show on October 29. At the moment, I am working with my collaborator on my autobiography, and we hope to have it published by Doubleday, in the spring in the states. Busy times!

Bless you and every good wish to you. -
Joan.

Joan's first biography, *A Portrait of Joan* was released in 1962.

October 17, 1961.

Dear Walter,

Thank you for your good letter. I hope you are having great success with your 'IDEAS' and that all is going well with you. Maria Fletcher is a charming, beautiful girl, with impeccable manners, and I was rooting for her from the beginning. I am so happy that she won. She has a brilliant future ahead of her, as she is beautiful and talented and gracious.
- Joan Crawford.

December 31, 1961.

My dear Larry,

How wonderful you were to demonstrate your friendship by the beautiful article you wrote about me in 'Hollywood Tattler.' I found the entire magazine so interesting - the Kim Novak story, "Bob Wagner's rebound from Natalie Wood" - Troy Donahue's story was of great interest to me because we are all asked questions about that incident. I was fascinated by the article, "Do Foreign Sex Films Menace Our Youths' Morals?"

I was delighted to have news on Alain Delon. The picture of Sandra Dee, Bobby Darin and the new baby is enchanting. Thank you again for being so wonderful to me. I am deeply grateful to you, and I hope your New Year will be tremendously successful and happy.
- Gratefully, Joan.

An undated letter written to Joan's ex neighbor, 'Annette Gordon of 23-G' and slipped under her apartment door reads as follows:

Dear Mrs. Gordon,

We are doing public service recordings and all we can hear is your daughter's yelling and tantrums. Is there no way you can control her? We would be so grateful if you would at least try. Why not try Central Park where she could draw a crowd?

- Joan Crawford.

This is perhaps the most toxic letter in the entire book. I wonder what Mrs. Gordon's reaction was to this letter?

March 24, 1962 - To Mrs. Frances Spingold

Frances, my darling -

I loved your sweet letter, and I am glad you will be coming home soon. I am sorry it hasn't been a good season for you there, but you must take it easy. I have just returned from Los Angeles, San Francisco and Honolulu, for Pepsi-Cola: and also a quick trip to Akron, Ohio, where I commentated a fashion show and helped out in some civic charities.

Now I am off to the country with the children, for their spring vacation. Unfortunately, they couldn't come home for my birthday yesterday, but will arrive today; and we are going to Westhampton on Monday, for a week; before I go off to Los Angeles again, to present the best actor's award at the Academy Awards show on April 9th. Let me hear from you somewhere along the line, my darling.

- With all my love, always, Joan.

As mentioned in her letter, Joan presented the Best Actor Oscar at the 1962 Academy Awards Ceremony. Maximillian Schell won for his role in, *Judgment at Nuremberg.*

June 17, 1962.

Shirley dear,

Thank you for your sweet wire. It arrived just as my children and I were having barbecued chicken and spare ribs at Beachcomber's. It made me so happy that I lost my appetite for my dinner, and I just reveled in your friendship. Bless you, and my love to you and your fella'.

- Joan.

JOAN CRAWFORD

April 30, 1962

Dear Allan,

Thank you so much for the lovely
birthday card and your letter. How
sweet you were to remember the date,
and I am deeply grateful to you.

We are still in the talking stage
about "What Ever Happened to Baby
Jane?" and "The Idol". I really
don't know whether or not I will make
the two films. It does look possible,
though, that I will make "Baby Jane"
in the summer in Hollywood.

Bless you, and my thanks for helping to make my birthday so happy.

June 30, 1962.

Dear Allan,

Thank you for your good letter, and all of your kind remarks about welcoming me home, and about the party at Lucey's. Aren't you sweet to say you are purchasing two copies of "A Portrait of Joan". The May Company Wilshire is holding and "Autograph Party" for me on Friday, July 6th, from 2.30 to 3.30, in case you would like to purchase them there and have them autographed.

I am sending an Engstead photograph to you under separate cover that I hope you will like. Bless you and thank you again.

- Joan Crawford.

July 2, 1962.

Dear Eugene,

Thank you so much for your charming letter. How nice to hear from you. I have just made The Caretaker, with Robert Stack and Polly Bergen. Within the next few days I will start, Whatever Happened to Baby Jane?, with Bette Davis, and we will be working on that film for the rest of the summer. Bless you.

- Joan Crawford.

In *Conversations with Joan Crawford* by Roy Newquist, Joan Crawford spoke of her bittersweet time making the cult classic, *Whatever Happened to Baby Jane?* -

"Christ. I still have nightmares about it. I know why the picture shouldn't have been made, and I know why it had to be made. I was lonely, worse than lonely, bored out of my skull, and I needed the money. It was a good script, and Bob Aldrich had tremendous faith in it. Nobody would finance it; they didn't think either Bette Davis or I had the box-office pull to make it a success. Finally it did get financed, but on such a low budget we had to shoot it so quickly and improvise so many interiors and even exteriors, I felt as though we were filming a newsreel, not a movie. I was tense and nervous and desperately unhappy at the time, but probably nobody on the set or in any audience noticed this, because it was part of my character. The character I played, I mean.

I didn't go in blind, mind you. I knew that Bette had all the best scenes, that she could top me all along the way. I was a cripple, physically, and she was demented, mentally, and the mental always wins out on the screen. But we didn't feud the way the publicity people wanted us to. We weren't friends, but we got along, and the picture was finished, and I went

136

back to New York and Bette went back to Connecticut, of wherever the hell, and our paths didn't cross again."

In getting away from the topic of *Whatever Happened to Baby Jane?* For a brief moment, it is important to elaborate on one of Joan's statements regarding how her image is portrayed.

In an eerily prophetic way, Joan is looking to the future with the comment, *'I never wanted to be some sort of joke in fag circles...'* So, with that said, it is probably best that Joan didn't live to see the annual screenings of *Mommie Dearest* around the country, especially in San Francisco. This isn't your regular movie going audience, it is an audience primarily made up of drag queens, all of them made up to look like 'Joan Crawford' and all screaming, *'Christina, get me the axe!'* in perfect unison with Faye Dunaway in the movie.

At the end of the screening, Christina presents the best Joan look-a-like with a decorated wire coat hanger. In an online article entitled, *'Mommie Dearest in Drag,'* by Paul Festa, Christina tries to justify the meaning of this bizarre prize. *"My coat hanger doesn't have anything to do with the original trauma anymore,"* Christina explains, *"Like the film, the gesture steps so far over the line. And also, it's an acknowledgment of reality."*

In the weekend leading up to Christmas in San Francisco, *'Christmas with Christina Crawford'* sold out the 1500 seat capacity (on both days) at the Castro Theater. This live-singing drag revue show is a spoof on the real life 1944 Christmas Eve at the Crawford mansion. For the sixth consecutive year, *'Christmas with the Crawfords'* has played to full houses for it's entire six-week duration. Because of the popularity of this annual San Francisco show, Joan Crawford has actually 'replaced' Santa Claus as the most recognized symbol of Christmas!

In getting back to *Baby Jane*, in *Bette Davis Speaks* by Boze Hadley, Bette discusses and reminisces about her experiences with Joan Crawford on, *Whatever Happened to Baby Jane?* In true Davis fashion, she pulls no punches, reveling in the fact that she's (at the time of this interview) lived almost eleven years longer than Joan, and can now spill the beans on any topic without a scathing 'Joan Crawford' note being written to her the very next day.

Bette Davis was far less 'politically (and socially) correct' than Joan. Here's yet another one of her candid comments on her memories of working with *the* Joan Crawford. In explaining Joan's withering appearance in *Baby Jane*, Bette Davis wonders how a starving woman's breasts can increase in size whilst the rest of her fades away.

"Christ! - You never know what size boobs that broad has strapped on! She must have a different set for each day.of the week! She's

supposed to be shriveling away, but her tits keep growing. I keep running into them, like the Hollywood Hills."

So much has been written about the infamous Crawford/Davis feud. Their eventual coming together on *Baby Jane* was the climax to decades of snide comments being flung in social and media circles. It was inevitable that this film, good or bad, would be considered a 'cult classic.' With that casting, how could it be considered anything else? Their decades of personal clashes suddenly became the ultimate publicity tool. As an audience we watch, fixated, as Bette Davis revels in her mental and physical torture of Joan, knowing full well, she's loving every single minute of it!

July 12, 1962 - To Mrs. Frances Spingold - Two-page letter on imprinted, "Joan Crawford" stationery.

Frances darling,

I loved your letter -- but you know me -- I wouldn't think of selling my blessed apartment at 2 East 70th Street. Please tell the lady that she is sweet -- but "No!" - I'm so happy for you that the market is doing better. Every time I hear of such good reports, I think of you.

Aren't you an angel to read my story in the Mirror. I am so grateful that you would do that. By the way, I just heard today that my book is on the bestseller list in the Los Angeles area this week. I never expected that!

Please do thank Lewis Stephenson for me for sending me the two photo static copies of Mr. Aversa's bill. It was very thoughtful of him. God bless you, my love. Take good care.

- As ever, Joan.

On the same day that she wrote this letter, Joan appeared on NBC's television show, *Your First Impression*.

July 23rd, 1962, was the first day of filming on *Whatever Happened to Baby Jane?*, Joan arrived on time, fifteen minutes prior to her on set call time of 9AM. She had a complete entourage consisting of her own hairdresser; make up artist, maid, secretary and chauffeur.

August 14, 1962 - On 'Joan Crawford' letterhead notepaper - To Mrs. Frances Spingold, Joan talks of her admiration for the professionalism of 'Bette Davis' and of the tight shooting schedule on *Whatever Happened to Baby Jane?* -

Frances, my love,

I talked to Terry, my secretary in New York, and she said you had called. I was delighted that you had missed me enough to take the time out of your busy day to call me. I'm so happy for you that the market is better now. I know you were terribly worried.

The film is coming along magnificently. I think it's the best job I have ever done, but then that's easy to do when you work with real pros such as Bette Davis and Bob Aldrich. The thirty-day shooting schedule isn't easy with a production this size, but we are aiming to make it.

I miss you very much -- miss talking with you - miss being close by -- but with the difference in time, it's so difficult to know when to call you. I send my love, my darling Frances. My present plans are to be back in New York on September 8th.

- God bless - Joan.

Joan was never a lover of sweets but her character, Blanche Hudson, in *Baby Jane* consumed quite a few chocolates during the course of the film. Joan complied with the script but compromised by making tiny bite sized meatballs in place of the sweets she was supposed to be indulging in on screen. In a black and white film, it's impossible for the audience to distinguish the difference between chocolates and mini meatballs. Joan was satisfied, and Blanche Hudson appeared to be a lifelong chocoholic!

August 25, 1962 - On 'Joan Crawford' notepaper - To Mrs. Frances Spingold .

Frances Darling,

I loved your letter. I'm glad to know that you are well. Yes, darling, the article on Bob Huffines Jr. is the one we know. I know what you mean about Mrs.Lavan. As usual, everything is just for show. I'm so glad you sent me a gossipy letter. It's just divine.

I loved the paragraph you circled about Earl Blackwell and Hong Kong. No wonder I have always wanted to go to the Orient. I knew it would be as heavenly as it sounds. I'm glad the stock market is better, and some of your worries are over.

The film with Bette Davis will be finished a week from Wednesday, and the twins and I will return to New York on September 8th. I will call you the moment I arrive. Don't bother to answer this, darling.

The children have returned from camp, and I have much, much packing to do for them and for me. I love you dearly, and will see you very soon now.

- Joan.

August 29, 1962 - To Candy Williams, Los Angeles, California.

Dear Candy -

Thank you for your most recent card and letter. I would love to see some photos of your new house, do send them to me next time you write. I may be able to give you some suggestions on what colorings to choose for your living room rug, so be sure to send me a photo of that particular room, won't you. I do love to decorate.

The last few months have been very busy. I'm sure you've already heard that I'm working on a new film with Bette Davis, directed by Robert Aldrich. It's a very unusual story and I think the public will enjoy seeing it. It's unlike anything I've ever done, or seen for that matter. I do hope you'll see it and let me know what you think of it, Candy.

I can hardly believe I've been making pictures for close to forty years! I still love it. Not many people can say that about a job they've had for that long, right?

I look forward to seeing your new house and at least giving you my opinion on interior designs and colors. Bless you.

- Much love, Joan.

On September 12, 1962, filming wrapped on *Whatever Happened to Baby Jane?* - On October 1, 1962, Joan promoted the film by appearing as the inaugural guest on the legendary, *The Tonight Show With Johnny Carson.*

October 20, 1962. - To persons unknown, relating to her upcoming film releases - In part...

Thank you so much for sending me the invitation to Marilyn's wedding. I'm sure it was a beautiful wedding and I do wish I could have been there. As you know, this has been an extremely busy summer for me, as I made two films. One - 'The Caretakers', with Robert Stack, Polly Bergen and Herbert Marshall - will be released early next year; and the other film, 'Whatever Happened to Baby Jane?' with Bette Davis, will be released in November. I hope you see the pictures, and find them entertaining.

In an undated handwritten letter, on imprinted "Cathy Crawford" stationery, a young Cathy writes a thank you note to Mrs. Frances Spingold - Since she mentions Thanksgiving dinner within the body of the letter, it helps to place this piece around late November, or early December. I estimate the year to be approximately, 1962.

To Frances Spingold from Cathy Crawford -

Dear Aunt Frances -
Thank you very much for inviting us to your lovely home for dinner last night. It was wonderful seeing you again and meeting the rest of your family. Thank you so much for the beautiful gold watches. You were so sweet to give them to us. I hope you enjoyed your Thanksgiving and thank you for making ours so happy.
- Love, Cathy.

Joan was adamant that her children maintain their own correspondence, insisting they write their own thank you notes, etc... This rare handwritten letter from Cathy Crawford, is a fine example of a good mother teaching her young daughter, "the right thing to do."

December 16, 1962 - To Mrs. Frances Spingold, on imprinted, "Seasons Greetings" stationery.

Frances dearest,
How good it was to talk to you, and I finally received your letter. I am glad you are in Florida where it is warmer for you. I am glad the doctor only comes once a week, which means you are better. I have missed you very, very much these long months I have been traveling. Sorry I cannot be there for the opening of Lawrence of Arabia, but I will be with the children in the country.
I love you so much, dear Frances. I will let you know if I can visit you as soon as the Holidays are over and I get the children back in school.
- Always, Joan (handwritten).

February 11, 1963 - To Mrs. Frances Spingold -

Frances darling,
I adored your sweet, loving letter. It was waiting for me upon my return from Jamaica yesterday, and it was a wonderful welcome. I had a fabulous rest, and am all suntanned, and feel fine again, and I'm now all ready for the rat race. Incidentally, it has started! - I am leaving today for Washington, D.C; and it's a business trip for Pepsi Cola. I'll be back in New York tomorrow and then I expect I'll be here for two or three months, as the workmen will need that time to repair this poor, sad, water-logged apartment. It was drying out while I was in Jamaica.
God bless, darling, and I send you my dearest love. When will you be coming back to New York?
- As ever, always Joan (handwritten).

141

As with much of the correspondence between Joan and Mrs. Spingold, this letter and a number of future letters, have Joan's letter along with Mrs. Spingold's response, or vice versa. It certainly helps to piece things together more easily when the initial letter, along with the recipients reply are found together.

March 14, 1963 - To Mrs. Frances Spingold - Two pages.

Frances, my darling,

Thank you for your beautiful, beautiful letter and for the wonderful clippings about you. You look fabulous and wonderful and happy and relaxed. It was such a joy talking with you, darling. I would suggest you call Allied Maintenance Company in New York. Their telephone number is:PE. 6-6000. Ask to speak to Mr. Frye or Mr. Cooper. These are the people who run Allied Maintenance. But ask for Mr. Yunka to supervise the cleaning of your home before you return.

Who knows where to hang your pictures, darling? You certainly should have someone from Sam Salz Gallery to supervise the hanging, because Sam knows where every picture goes. Don't, under any circumstances, allow anyone in your home with all those paintings, without having someone from the Gallery there at the same time. Those paintings are too valuable!

I am sad that I can't visit you this season, but we will get together next year. I am enclosing my itinerary, darling. I will call you just as soon as I get to New York.

- Love, Joan.

March 21, 1963 - Mrs. Frances Spingold's reply to Joan's above letter is gushing with warmth, love and enthusiasm. She tells Joan that she's a blessing to her soul and although she dearly relishes her letters, she mustn't overdo it. She works too hard and if she can't write often, she certainly understands.

Of particular interest is a newspaper article that she says she will be enclosing that implies that Joan may become the wife of *"our Governor."* She of course compliments Joan by telling her than no lady could ever grace a room like, *"my Joan"* and that if the newspaper prediction were to come true, she truly would be *"first lady of the land."* She humorously states that if Joan does become First Lady, *"we can tell Jackie (Kennedy) to go back to Boston or wherever she lives..."*

With the absence of the above mentioned article from the West Palm Beach newspaper. I can only assume the article of which Mrs. Spingold refers is in relation to a possible relationship between Joan and Nelson Rockefeller. Mrs. Spingold is jumping ahead of herself in having

142

Joan become the new Mrs. Nelson Rockefeller, and subsequently the *"First Lady of the Land,"* but she was surely the best rallier that Joan had for that possibility.

March 22, 1963 - On "Helen Norfleet Individual Study Programs" letterhead. A letter from Miss Helen Norfleet to Mrs. Frances Spingold, in relation to Cathy's enrollment in her program. Miss Norfleet asks for a reference from her detailing Cathy's abilities, disposition and home background.

March 28, 1963 - Mrs. Frances Spingold responds to Miss Norfleet's letter regarding Cathy Crawford. She states that she knows both children (Cathy and Cindy) and they are both well-behaved girls and outstanding pupils. She says that Cathy is an obedient girl and if it is her desire to enter the school program, the school would be lucky to have such a nice girl. She ends her letter by praising Joan's expert parenting and guidance of her children.

It seems Mrs. Spingold's letter to Miss Norfleet convinced the school to accept both Cathy and Cindy into their program. The following letter is from Joan -

June 10, 1963 - To a teacher in charge of summer camp for twins, Cathy and Cindy.

Dear Miss Norfleet,

Enclosed are the following forms on Cindy and Cathy for enrollment in your camp:

Application form, Payments for extras form, Tuition refund coverage.

Also enclosed is my check in the amount of $1,591.50 ($795.75 for each one), which includes the following:

Tuition (June 25 - Aug. 20) - $700.00
Payment for extras   77.50
Additional insurance   4.00
Travel expenses (bus to camp) 14.25

Total - $795.75 each

I haven't included any funds for tutoring or private lessons because we will have to wait until the girls get to camp before we know just what they need and what they will be interested in taking. But for Cindy, speech is definite. She must have tutoring every day - also spelling is a must for her. Naturally, Cathy will be taking art. Both girls are definitely in need of ballet for posture and grace and I do hope they will take it.

The girls will bring the 'Campers Health Examination Form' with them when they go to camp, also the 'Medical Reimbursement Insurance' form.

- Sincerely, Joan Crawford.

August 6, 1963 - To Mrs. Frances Spingold on "Joan Crawford" stationery - The "picture" she is referring to in the letter is, "Straight Jacket" -

Frances darling,

Thank you so much for your dear, sweet letter. I hope you are feeling well. I'm so happy that you have been watching my pictures on late night television. The picture is coming along beautifully. The cast and crew are wonderful, and we are having a ball. I think this is the happiest, most congenial crew I've ever worked with. And it really shows - in the "rushes."

I will be back in New York on the 25th. I'm longing to see you. I'm delighted you have finished with the dentist. I love you dearly, and I think you will be very happy with the picture.

- All my love - Joan.

August 9, 1963 - Typed letter on personal letterhead to a friend in relation to her latest film project. - In part...

I am making a film, 'Straight Jacket', at Columbia Studios, with Leif Erickson and Diane Baker. The script was written by Robert Bloch, who wrote 'Psycho,' and it's unusual and full of suspense. I think you will find it a real shocker!

The sound effects for the decapitation scenes in *Straight Jacket (1964)* were made by the prop man cutting watermelons in half. Columbia Pictures even joined in the theme of things with their familiar lady with the torch logo. She appears at the end of the film, as usual, only this time her head is missing!

Ex-husband Franchot Tone proposed to Joan (again!) over the phone during the production. When she failed to respond, he knew the answer was...no!

September 7, 1963 - To gossip columnist 'Shirley Eder' -

Shirley Darling,
Thank you so much for sending me all the clippings -- all that beautiful publicity! - You are a blessed angel. Please forgive this brief note, honey, I am up to my "A---" in 'Route 66', here in Poland Spring, Maine. I'll return to New York on the 15th.
- Love, as ever - Joan.

January 29, 1964.

My dear David Jackson,
Thank you so much for your charming letter and for the photographs which I have signed and which, I am sure , you have by now. How good of you to send a return stamped envelope for my convenience. It is very rare for people to be so considerate and I thank you. I hope you don't mind and won't think me presumptuous if I send you a new picture.
- Gratefully, Joan Crawford.

January 31, 1964.

Alta dear,
Thank you so much for coming to our press conference, and for being so gracious and charming to me. I'm very glad that I stayed in Boston long enough to see your review of 'Straight-Jacket' and your interview with me in the Boston Traveler.
Usually I leave the cities so fast, and I don't get any of the printed publicity until two to three weeks later. But this time, I had the joy of reading your nice comments, and I am so grateful to you. Bless you, and my deepest salaams for your graciousness and your kindness to me.
- Love, Joan.

In the book, *Conversations with Joan Crawford*, Joan talks about her choice of films after the highly successful, *Whatever Happened To Baby Jane?* - "*They were all terrible, even the few I thought might be good. I made them because I needed the money (she was paid $50,000 plus a percentage of profits) or because I was bored or both. I hope they've been exhibited and withdrawn and are never heard from again.*"

February 8, 1964 - Typed letter on "Joan Crawford" imprinted stationary.

My dear Doug -
I am so delighted you liked "Straight Jacket" - Thank you for your wonderfully descriptive letter, and for being so observant too! - I'm deeply grateful for all of your wonderful words of praise. Yes, I'll make "Whatever Happened to Cousin Charlotte?" in May, but I'm not going to tell you the plot yet! - I want you to be surprised. We haven't cast the other parts yet.
Bless, you and thank you again for your friendship and loyalty. Hope I will see you again soon, as it would give me great joy. I'm in Jamaica at the moment, having a much-needed rest. I'll return to New York around the end of February.

- Joan.

The name of the film she'll be working on in May - *Whatever Happened to Cousin Charlotte?,* went on to become, *Hush, Hush Sweet Charlotte* - The events surrounding this film and Joan's non appearance, is explained in future correspondence.

March 7, 1964 - To 'Missy' aka Barbara Stanwyck.

Missy Darling,
I have been waiting to write to you when I could do a long hand letter, but there just never comes that time. Your Santa Claus card this past Christmas was just adorable, and you were sweet to think of me.
Your book is here and your autograph is so warm and loving. I am deeply grateful to Nolan for getting it for me, and to you for autographing it so sweetly. I must say, darling, when people come to see me, the book is picked up by them and I never see their faces the rest of the evening, they are buried in the book! It is magnificently done and you must be very happy with it. I received your note today too, about the wire that I sent to you. God bless and my dearest love to you.

- Joan.

April 2, 1964 - To Mrs. Frances Spingold on "Joan Crawford" imprinted stationery.

Frances darling,
Thank you so much for your lovely letter and the sweet, sweet birthday telegram. I'm so grateful to you. I'm glad you are coming back to New York. I will only be here until April 4th, however, darling, and am then going to Los Angeles and will fly to Honolulu on April 14th.

The girls are back in school now. Cindy had to have her wisdom teeth extracted, and was in the hospital overnight, but is feeling fine now, thank goodness. Darling, do call me the minute you arrive in New York. I hope to see you before I leave on the 4th.

You are such a dear friend. I hope you will be happy in your new apartment. I'm sorry I haven't had a chance to see it yet. I'll be back in New York the end of April for a few days, for annual meetings and board meetings for Pepsi, etc., and then I will head out to California to make the new picture. You are an angel to remember my birthday, darling.

- Love, always Joan.

May 6, 1964 - Typed letter to, "J. Charles Grant," Joan's Houseman for many years.

My dear Mr. Grant -

Thank you so much for the Mother's Day card. What a beautiful one it is, indeed. The colors just match those in my bedroom. I'm off to California next week to do, 'Hush, Hush Sweet Charlotte.' Will be about three months on the picture, then do some overseas traveling for Pepsi, so won't be back until next fall. Hope to see you then. Again, my grateful thanks for remembering me.

-Gratefully, Joan Crawford.

May 26, 1964 - To Mrs. Frances Spingold -

Frances darling,

How sad I am that I didn't get to see you before I left for New York, but you what a heavy schedule I had. We are rehearsing now, and have many problems, but I hope they will be solved soon. I'm leaving on location on Saturday for Baton Rouge, Louisiana, and we will probably be there about ten days. My dearest love to you -- and I hope you are feeling well. When are you moving into your new apartment?

- Love, as ever - Joan.

The "many problems" that Joan is referring to in the above letter were happening on the set of the ill fated (at least for Joan), *Hush...Hush, Sweet Charlotte.*

June 7, 1964 - To Mrs. Frances Spingold -

Frances darling,

Your letter came to me on location, and I was so pleased to hear from you. I know that moving to your new apartment is a very difficult decision to make. I know it would be a chore, but I think you will be much happier in the long run to get out from the burden of the big house and all the staff problems. By the time you receive this, I will be back in Los Angeles, as I am flying back on Tuesday. My dearest, dearest love to you, darling.

- Always, Joan.

June 15, 1964 - TELEGRAM - From Mrs. Frances Spingold, to Joan, care of "Cedars of Lebanon Hospital", Hollywood, California. This get well telegram was sent to Joan on one of her hospital stays during the initial production stages of, *Hush...Hush, Sweet Charlotte.*

PLEASE, DARLING, GET WELL SOON. WE ALL LOVE YOU SO VERY DEARLY. I WISH I COULD DO SOMETHING FOR YOU. FRANCES SPINGOLD.

June 18, 1964 - WESTERN UNION TELEGRAM - From Joan, in response to the above get well telegram from Mrs. Frances Spingold.

FRANCES DARLING, THANK YOU SO MUCH FOR YOUR WIRE. HOPE TO BE OUT OF HOSPITAL THIS WEEK. IT WAS WITHIN ONE INCH OF GOING INTO PNEUMONIA. THAT'S WHY THEY PUT ME HERE, MAYBE ONE OF THESE DAYS I'LL LEARN NOT TO WORK SO HARD. LOVE JOAN.

June 18, 1964 - Mrs. Frances Spingold responds to Joan's above telegram, the same afternoon by telling her that she's praying that she stops working so hard. She advises her to cut back her workload and make one picture every now and then. She tells her that she is so full of worry about her that she simply can't sleep.

July 29, 1964 - To Mrs. Frances Spingold - Amidst the catastrophes of , *Hush...Hush, Sweet Charlotte.*

Frances, my love -
Thank you so much - I adore the picture of us - and thank you too for the dear, sweet note.
I've been working in front of the cameras a few hours every day, and I am feeling stronger each day. My dearest love to you - and I promise to take it easy, especially since I just walked in the door and found your exquisite white chrysanthemums. How dear and sweet you were to want to share them with me, and they are truly magnificent. I'm so deeply grateful to you, my darling.

- Love, Joan.

Undated, 1964 - Mrs. Frances Spingold's responds to Joan's above letter telling her how sorry she is that she's back in the hospital again. She says that Leo Jaffe phoned her the night before last, to tell her that "her Joan" had been replaced by Loretta Young on the picture. She praised Loretta Young as an actress but goes on to say that she is "no Joan Crawford."

August 12, 1964 - On blue 'Joan Crawford' notepaper - Typed from her hospital bed after collapsing on the set of, *Hush...Hush, Sweet Charlotte.*

Frances darling,

I adored your letter of August 6. It was in the newspaper that Loretta Young had been asked to replace me, but she has refused the role, so at the moment there is no replacement. It would be a blessing if they would replace me, as I must take a month's rest after I leave the hospital.

The twins are in Newport, Rhode Island, at summer school, and they will be there only until the 22nd of the month. What have you decided to do about the apartment? - I know it would have been impossible for you to have moved during this awful heat wave. My dearest, dearest love to you.

- Joan.

The above collection of letters refer to Joan's 'illness' and subsequent withdrawal from the film, *Hush...Hush, Sweet Charlotte.* The pairing of Joan Crawford and Bette Davis on the heels of the success of *Whatever Happened To Baby Jane?* was a sure fire recipe for yet another cult classic.

With a working title of *Whatever Happened To Cousin Charlotte?* Henry Farrell, the same novelist who penned, *Baby Jane*, wrote the story. This time he wrote with Joan and Bette in mind to star in his finished tome.

However customized the story was for the actresses, it just wasn't meant to be. It is said that Joan got so worked up emotionally about the thought of working with Bette Davis again; she fell apart, literally, and checked herself into Cedars Sinai Hospital. Upon returning to the set, she complained constantly of fatigue and after barely working half a day, she left, not one, not two, but four days running. Director, Robert Aldrich, warned Joan that her consistence absences from the set were going to result in legal action by the pictures insurance company. His threats did little to persuade her to stay on, she found Bette Davis' bully tactics too much to bear, returning to hospital and halting production once more.

On August 3rd, 1964, Joan was rushed by ambulance to Cedars Sinai Hospital, for the third time. It was ten days later that she heard of her replacement via a radio broadcast playing in her hospital room. With a salary of $100,000 plus bonuses (almost double Joan's deal for the same role), Olivia De Havilland agreed to replace her.

Joan was not only released from the picture, she was released from the hospital soon after the announcement of her replacement was made. Joan told former lover, director and author, Vincent Sherman, how she heard of her replacement - *"I heard the news of my replacement over the radio, lying in my hospital bed. I wept for thirty-nine hours.... I still believe in this business, but there should be some gentleness. I think it takes a lot of guts to make pictures, and I'm going to make a lot more of them. But I am going to make them with decent, gentle people."*

August 13, 1964 - To Mrs. Frances Spingold on Joan Crawford imprinted stationery, regarding the impending induction of Columbia Pictures Vice-President, Leo Jaffe as a Fellow of Brandeis University - The letter is a form letter to all invitees, with handwritten name and signature.

Frances, my love (handwritten) -

My very good friend, Leo Jaffe, executive vice-president of Columbia Pictures Corporation, will be inducted as a Fellow of Brandeis University at a National Dinner of Entertainment Industry to be held on October 5, 1964.

The Dinner, which will take place in New York, will provide the opportunity for the University to express its appreciation to Mr. Jaffe for the leadership and support he is giving to the development at Brandeis of one of the finest Entertainment Arts schools in the country. The program will be built around the Nate B. and Frances Spingold Theatre Arts Center now being constructed on the University campus.

Though I have been given the imposing title of General Chairman of this dinner, please understand that its business-like formality in no way expresses my personal enthusiasm and hopes for this fine event.

I am organizing a National Committee of Sponsors and would like very much to include your name on this Committee. The work involved for you personally will be nominal, but by lending your name to the sponsor list the respect and regard it engenders should contribute immeasurably to the success of the Dinner.

Please write me at my home, 2 East 70th Street, New York City and tell me of your acceptance. I will be looking forward to having you join us in planning this memorable event.

- Always, Joan (handwritten).

PS: Please mark the date on your calendar.

August 27, 1964 - To "Dore Freeman" of MGM Studios.

Enclosed with this letter was Joan's hospital I.D bracelet, used during her stay at "Cedars of Lebanon Hospital" during the filming of Hush...*Hush, Sweet Charlotte* -

Dore dear -
 I just came out of the hospital this morning - and I didn't forget that you want my "bracelet" - so here it is. Bless you and my love to you and Bill.

- Joan.

September 28, 1964 - Brandeis University Letterhead - To Mrs. Frances Spingold, and signed by her. A copy of which would be then printed and sent out as a follow up on Joan's above letter to all invitees.

Dear Mrs. Spingold -
 Recently you received an invitation to attend a Dinner which will induct Mr. Leo Jaffe, Executive Vice President of Columbia Pictures Corporation, as a Fellow of Brandeis University.
 As you know, Joan Crawford is Chairman of the Dinner. The Dinner is a national affair, under the sponsorship of prominent persons in our Industry, many of whom have already reserved for the Dinner.
 This marvelous tribute to Leo Jaffe, which is being given to him by this fine young University is deserving of our participation. He has worked so hard for so many communities and for many, many causes in our Industry.
 A wonderful program is being arranged which I know you will enjoy. Won't you honor Leo Jaffe and Joan Crawford by attending this interesting dinner. The cost is a nominal $25.00 per person. I hope I will have the opportunity to see you there.
 - Affectionately, Frances Spingold.

September 25, 1964 - To Mrs. Frances Spingold.

Frances darling,
 Thank you so much for my beautiful white chrysanthemums. How dear you were to have greeted me so generously and glamorously on my return home. I'm longing to see you. Let me know when you have a moment. My dearest love to you -
 - Always, Joan - (handwritten).

September 30, 1964 - Mrs. Frances Spingold's responds to Joan's above letter with the same devotion as usual. She tells Joan not to thank her for anything because no matter what she does, it is simply not enough. "I would like to be at your feet," she says. She asks that Joan try and attend her party, so that she can "grace the entire affair as the queen of the world."

November 4, 1964 - To gossip columnist, Shirley Eder.

Shirley Darling,
You were an angel to send me the two copies of your column, and to put me in headlines -- and to write such lovely things about me too! - I'm so grateful. I'm sorry we missed each other telephonically on Sunday, Darling.
The picture is going well. Bill Castle and Don and all send you their love. I am giving a party for the two teenagers at the Studio on Friday. I wish you could join us. This is the 'happiest' company - we have a divine and well-selected crew...........the best in the business.
My love to you, dear friend. When will you be in California? I'm going to Chicago on Tuesday until the 14th, then back here, and to Palm Springs for Thanksgiving. At least these are my plans for the moment.
- Love, as ever, Joan.

January 22, 1965 - USO of New York City "Woman of the Year" Luncheon, honoring, "Joan Crawford" - This is a form letter, sent to Mrs. Frances Spingold, informing her of the upcoming luncheon honoring Joan as "Woman of the Year" for 1965.

Dear Mrs. Spingold -
We take great pleasure in announcing that Joan Crawford has been chosen to receive the USO of New York City's 1965 "Woman of the Year" Award for her outstanding contribution to the morale and welfare of America's men and women in uniform.
Mary Martin and the Committee cordially invite you to join us at our gala luncheon on March 2nd at the Plaza Grand Ballroom when outstanding personalities of the theater business world will gather to honor Miss Crawford.
Women have always played a leading role in promoting USO, and through this tribute to Joan Crawford we are also expressing our grateful appreciation to the thousands of women volunteers who daily serve in USO clubs around the world.
The comedy team of Allen & Rossi and Metropolitan Opera star Blanche Thebom, among others, will headline an exciting program of

entertainment. Because a large attendance is expected, we hope you will send in your reservation on the enclosed form as soon as possible, since all reservations will be made in the order received. Looking forward to seeing you at the luncheon -

- Sincerely - Mrs. Mary G. Roebling and
Mrs. Walter S. Mack - Co-Chairman.

February 22, 1965 - TELEGRAM - Western Union - To Frances Spingold, from, Joan Crawford.

FRANCES DARLING. LOVED YOUR LETTER. DO HOPE YOU CAN BE PRESENT AT USO LUNCHEON BUT DONT JEOPARDIZE YOUR HEALTH IN ANY WAY. IF YOU NEED THE REST IN PALM BEACH I WILL CERTAINLY UNDERSTAND. ALL MY LOVE - JOAN.

February 24, 1965 - Mrs. Frances Spingold responds to Joan's above telegram regretfully informing her that she is not well and will not be able to make her "Woman of the Year" dinner. She asks for her forgiveness for not attending and assures her that her heart will be with her for every second on that special day. She ends her letter asking for some newspaper clippings of the event and finally says, "I am glad the world realizes they have my Joan."

March 24, 1965 - To Mrs. Frances Spingold -

Frances darling,
Your wire is the most beautiful one I have ever received, and thank you more that I can possibly say for remembering my birthday in such a lovely manner. I too will be so happy to see the Joan Crawford Dancing School at Brandeis University. When you have the time, darling, do send me your new apartment address. Do you have the phone number yet? God bless, and my dearest love to you. I will be in California until April 6, then to North California for Pepsi, and back in New York on April 10.

- Love, as ever – Joan.

May 24th, 1966.

Dear Hy,
So sorry to have missed seeing you on Saturday evening. Franchot and I had supper at Voison and not only toasted you with your gift of champagne but brought the rest of the bottle home with us. Bless you.

- Joan.

153

August 17th, 1966.

Dear Rosalie,

Thank you for your very nice letter and for your best wishes to Christina on her marriage. She has married a wonderful young man, and they are blissfully happy - and so am I, for them. They are living in New York at the present time.

I'm glad you liked me on "Hollywood Palace" - I'm going to do another one in a few months and it will be shown on television on March 4, 1967, and I'll hope you'll enjoy this one too. Also, I am going to make a film for Columbia Pictures this fall titled, 'Circus of Blood.' At least that is the tentative title, but I expect it will be changed. It is not a horror film. The script is fantastic, and I am very excited about it.

Bless you and I hope you are having a wonderful simmer.

- Joan.

A remake of the 1937 film, *The Shadow*. The working title of the cult classic, *Berserk,* was *Circus of Blood,* also known as, *Circus of Terror.* Joan's salary was a flat $55,000. The British press gave Joan the title, "Her Serene Crawfordship."

She would arrive at least two hours before her call time every morning to cook breakfast for the entire crew. Even after all her years of being a movie star, she was always comfortable in mixing with the common folk, the ordinary worker, and she did not see it beneath her to do so.

Pepsi was the drink of choice and free to anyone who cared to drink it on the set, but workers would only receive a new bottle when they returned their empty one. An avid recycler, Joan's was quoted as saying, *"You'd be surprised at how much money we lose on unreturned empties."*

September 6, 1966 - To a 'Mr. Lee McWilliams' of Urbana, Ohio.

Dear Lee,

How kind and generous of you to send me such a lovely corsage while I was in Springfield, with your nice personal message of good wishes. I loved your beautiful fall colors, with all the jewels around them. It was most unusual and in excellent taste. Had a busy but very happy day - made even happier by your thought of me. Bless you and I do hope to have an opportunity to meet you and thank you in person some day.

- Joan.

December 9, 1966 - On Grosvenor House letterhead, onion skin paper - To Mrs. Frances Spingold, sent airmail, from London - The 'picture' she mentions is *Berserk!,* filmed entirely on location in the U.K. -

154

Frances darling -

How good is was to get your letter of November 29th. I have completed the picture, including dubbing and interviews, and am down now with a very bad cold. I am so sad that Leo is mad at you. I am sure if you could explain and tell him the truth he would understand. He is a very loyal friend of yours and devoted to you beyond belief. I hope by this time all is cleared up between you and him.

I hope all is going well in Palm Beach and that you are getting some rest and not overdoing the social bit. Is Doris still with you? Take good care. My dearest, dearest love to you, Frances.

- Always, Joan.

April 13, 1967 - To, "Sally Roberts" of New York.

Dear Sally,

Thank you very much for the warm and friendly birthday card. It was wonderful to hear from you again. That's the best part of birthdays, hearing from my old friends. Incidentally, I will be on "Hollywood Palace" on April 22. You may want to watch the show. I'll also be on Merv Griffin's Show on April 18. Bless you and I hope you are having a happy springtime.

- Always, Joan.

"Hollywood Palace" ran from January 1964 thru February 1970. A guest host presented the show each week. It was an unusual format that helped alleviate the possibility of audience boredom.

May 18, 1967 - To 'Shirley Eder' - Detroit Free Press.

Shirley, my darling,

Thank you for all the lovely things you wrote about me in your column of April 23rd, and about the Woman of the Year award and 'Hollywood Palace.' I wonder if I could have another copy or two of your column so that I could send them to the 'Hollywood Palace' people. It would make them so happy.

I've just returned from a week in Mexico City, attending the Variety Clubs International Convention and doing some work for Pepsi down there. It was all very exciting, and it's great to be home - but you know me, I'm knee-deep in packing again, and this time for Fort Smith, Arkansas, to attend a Pepsi plant opening, and then to Dallas, Texas in early June. God bless and my love to you and Edward.

- Joan.

May 23, 1967 -

Dear Gail,

Thank you for your very nice letter - I am so pleased that you enjoyed the 'Hollywood Palace' that I appeared on, and that you liked my reading of 'The Dreamer.' It is kind of you to want to write about me for the all-star-fan club. You asked if I enjoyed making movies in the 30's and 40's more than now.

Well, no, no actually. I've <u>always</u> enjoyed making movies. Now we work only five days a week at the Studio and in the 30's and 40's, we worked six days a week, so at least I have one more days rest for the next week's work. However, my day of rest is not spent resting, but in keeping up with my correspondence. Thank you again, for thinking of me.

- Joan Crawford.

Christmas, 1967 - On Seasons Greetings imprinted stationery -

Frances darling,

This Christmas greeting is sent with my deep gratitude for your friendship. May you enjoy all the happiness of Christmas, and may God's blessings be with you and your loved ones in the New Year.

- Love, Joan - (handwritten).

January 2, 1968 - To Mrs. Frances Spingold.

Frances darling,

I loved your letters. It was so good to talk with you on New Year's Day. I am delighted you are coming back for induction. I am off to California, as I told you. I'll be back in New York at the end of January. God bless - And I am looking forward to seeing you when you get to New York.

- Love, as ever - Joan.

January 18, 1968 - Mrs. Frances Spingold responds to Joan's above letter by telling her that whenever she receives a letter or a telephone call from her she feels "well all over." She tells Joan that everyone keeps asking about when she is coming there, "everyone adores you" she gushes.

March 12, 1968 - To "Holly Geetah of Holly Specialized Service - Dallas, Texas."

Dear Holly Geetah,
Thank you so very much for presenting me with the lovely personalized cocktail napkins during my appearance in Sanger-Harris. How nice of you to have them made up especially for me. They are such an attractive and useful gift and I'm so deeply grateful to you for your kindness. Bless you and the best of good wishes to you.
- Joan Crawford.

June 29, 1968. - On "Joan Crawford" imprinted letterhead

Thank you for your very nice letter. I am happy to know that you enjoyed seeing us on the Merv Griffin television show. It was sweet of you to be concerned about my ankles, Barbara. All is well now. I tore the ligaments from one ankle and sprained the other, but that accident happened in April, and they are fine now, and completely healed, and I am back 'on my feet'.
Yes, Christina Crawford is my daughter, and she plays, 'Joan' on 'The Secret Storm.' I think she is doing a lovely job of it too, and I am a very proud mother. Yes, I do read and answer my mail. I dictate my answers to my secretary. In fact, I spend many hours at my desk doing it! - So.........tell your friend...
I am sorry Barbara but I don't have any copies left of my autobiography. It is out of print now, and I really don't know where you would be able to buy a copy. Perhaps at a second hand bookstore. That's the best suggestion I have at the moment. If you do find a copy of it, you may send it to me and I will be happy to inscribe it for you and return it. Bless you. I hope you are having a happy summer -- and my best wishes to you and your friend.
- Joan Crawford.

Late June, 1968 - On Muscular Dystrophy Association Letterhead - With Joan being listed as the "Honorary Chairman, Theatre Benefit." A form letter, this one to Mrs. Frances Spingold.

Dear Friends -
Would you honor us by attending a very important event? I'm referring to a gala evening we're planning on Friday, October 25, 1968. The event is the showing of the year's most anticipated musical film -- STAR! -- based on the life of Gertrude Lawrence and starring Julie Andrews. The film will be shown at the Rivoli Theatre.

Please fill in the reservation card enclosed and return it to me as soon as possible. You'll be joining many other distinguished benefactors that evening! Your support of the event will make it possible for the Manhattan Chapter of MDAA to carry on its vital patient and community service programs. You'll be helping to provide the funds necessary to support our two local clinics, as well as the occupational therapy unit at MDAA's Institute for Muscle Disease. What else can I say, except that we -- and the patients we serve -- will be very, very grateful for your assistance
- Bless you - Joan Crawford.

July 3, 1968 - Mrs. Frances Spingold responds to Joan's above letter with a generous donation of $500.00. She also mentions how much she enjoyed spending the evening with Joan and Tina.

July 13, 1968 - To Mrs. Frances Spingold - Two pages -

Frances darling,
Loved your sweet letter and I'm so happy you enjoyed the evening with the Jaffes, Tina and me. It was so good to have you with us, but I do hope you weren't upset because I couldn't reach Mama at the apartment. You were a dear to be so concerned and to stop by, to make sure all was well.
We found everything just fine -- apparently, the phone hadn't rung or else Mama hadn't heard it. Dear, dear Frances -- I'm overwhelmed by your generosity to Muscular Dystrophy. What an angel you are to send $500.00, when there are so many other demands on you. Thank you, dear friend, from the bottom of my heart - and God bless.
Did you enjoy your weekend out of the city? Do hope so - the weather was so ideal. So much love, always - Will be talking to you soon.
- Joan.

"Mama" was a German immigrant and a mother of nine children. She was hired in the early sixties as Joan's maid and personal assistant. She apparently got the job after telling Joan that she enjoyed scrubbing floors on her hands and knees instead of using a mop. She was often referred to as Mamacita, or Mama for short, as in the above letter.

October 13, 1968 - To 'Shirley Eder' - Detroit Free Press.

Shirley dear,
Thank you for your sweet letter and for being so wonderful to me in your column. And thank you too for offering me the use of your

158

Presidential Suite - but it's no good without the President, by golly. What kind of hostess are you?

Darling, I don't even attempt to keep up with the Sinatras or believe the rumors about them. It would be and endless turmoil. But at least they are good copy. I think Nancy Jr. is as cute as a button - and Nancy Sr. is one of the loveliest ladies I've ever known. God bless - and my love to you.

- As ever, Joan.

November 26, 1968 - To gossip columnist 'Shirley Eder.'

Shirley love,

Thank you for your Xerox copy of your column mentioning me. You are a blessed lamb to write such nice things about Christina and me, and we are both very grateful. I was amused at your paragraph about Peter O'Toole. He's a strange one - but indeed a beautiful actor. God bless - and I hope that you and Edward have a happy Thanksgiving.

- Love, Joan.

April 29, 1969 - To Mrs. Frances Spingold.

Frances darling,

Thank you so much, my darling, for these glorious white chrysanthemums. They are just beautiful in my living room and, now that I'll be home for a while, I can really enjoy their beauty. You were dear to send them to me.

Do hope that you're feeling well and that the Florida heat isn't too much for you. I know you can really take it -- I would be just a grease pot in that kind of heat. Take care of yourself, dear heart. Will be in touch with you before I leave for London, shortly after the middle of May.

- So much love, Joan.

October 1, 1969 -

Mike dear,

Thank you so very much, Mike Dear, for my lovely silver dinner bell. All I have to do is to make a wish - and my wishes come true! - I didn't think you had even noticed my mention of a dinner bell on Monday evening. Just delighted to have it, and I need one very much, and this one is so pretty and dainty - I love it! - It was so dear and thoughtful of you to send it to me.

As for our financial relations, they are worse than the international debt: - Bless you for keeping such an accurate accounting,

159

but I'm sure it has all ended up to my advantage. It was so good seeing you - will be talking to you soon,

- Love, Joan.

December 20, 1969 - Two page letter on 'Joan Crawford' notepaper.

May Dear,

 Thank you for your sweet letter, the dear Christmas card to Cindy, Cathy and me: and for the clippings about the Garbo television show. I'm so glad you and some of your friends saw it and liked it. I've received such nice letters from people who saw it, but the press seemed needlessly critical, alas.

 I am <u>so</u> sorry to hear about your father's difficulty with his legs, and that you feel you can't leave home for more than an hour or two at a time. Would it be possible to have a practical nurse help at times, or a friend? You have always been so vibrant and active, and had so many interests in life. I do hope you will find a solution so that you can be 'out and about' sometime, May dear.

 I'm in Los Angeles at the moment, finishing a segment of 'The Virginian' for television. It will be shown here in the States on January 21. We have a lovely script, and I think it will turn out well. Do you watch much television? I know 'The Virginian' is shown in England, but I have no idea when this segment will be shown there.

 I'll be going to Sao Paulo, Brazil in late January for Pepsi-Cola, and I'm looking forward to that trip very much, as I've never been there, although have seen other parts of Brazil. Bless you, and I hope you and your father have a wonderfully happy Christmas and that 1970 will bring all that you desire.

- Love, Joan.

 Joan's part in "The 'Garbo' Television Show" was that of hostess and narrator.

The Letters...The Final Decade

"There is no need to hole up in an apartment and die alone. No. None. Poor Joan. I wish I could have liked her more."

- Bette Davis on Joan's death.

February 27, 1970.

Dear John Hughes,
Thank you so much for your very nice letter. It was kind of you to take the time to write to me. I am delighted to know of your interest in me, and your loyalty through the years. I'm happy too that you have enjoyed my performances on the screen. I am sending an autographed photo to you under separate cover that I hope you will like. All good wishes to you always.

- Joan Crawford.

February 26, 1971 - To 'Shirley Eder" of the 'Detroit Free Press' - In part...

You were sweet to explain so well about the Hollywood Foreign Press Award incident when I presented Frank Sinatra's award to Tina. And, dear friend, I wish Ross Hunter would make a Joan Crawford picture for Joan Crawford!

May 20, 1971 - To 'Lawrence J. Quirk' of New York, N.Y.

Larry dear,
How wonderful you were to drop off at my apartment house your new book - 'The Films Of Paul Newman.' I am so deeply gracious to you for your precious friendship and for your beautiful inscription.

It is lovely that you can now think of your mother without too much pain and can remember her beauty - beauty of mind and spirit. She still walks in it, you know. So glad things are looking 'up' for you at last, Larry dear, and do hope you and Frank have a wonderful trip to London. Please say 'hello' to Frank for me, and also to Michael Greenwood when you see him.

I think you would enjoy meeting Alexander Walker, who writes for the 'Evening Standard,' while you're in London. Other than you he has more knowledge about the movies than any other young man I know of. Enclosed is a copy of the letter I've written him about your visit. Thank you so much for including me in your next book, 'The Films of Frederic March' - God bless and love always.

- Joan.

June 14, 1971 - To persons unknown - In part...

I loved your sweet letter and all the divine things you had to say about me and my career. Now, about, 'Our Dancing Daughters' - none of us who made films at MGM was allowed to have a print of our films. I only wish I had a print of that and of all the movies I made at MGM.

August 25, 1971 - To 'Shirley Eder' of the 'Detroit Free Press', Detroit, Michigan.

Shirley Dear -
Thank you so much for all the clippings and for all the fine things you had to say about my visit to Detroit. You're quite right, dear friend. Suzy Farbman is a bitch: I'm not even going to write her.

Just returned from a trip to Birmingham, Alabama, for the American Film Institute. The good merchants of Birmingham gave 10,000 to the A.F.I., which I accepted for George Stevens, Jr. who was unable to be there.

Next stop will be Washington, D.C. for a 'Joan Crawford Film Festival' week sponsored by the A.F.I. Then off to San Francisco and back to Birmingham again - for Pepsi. Much love. I'll keep in touch.

- Always, Joan.

162

One of the last publicly released photographs taken of Joan with her beloved Shih Tzu, Princess.

October 18, 1971 - To 'Shirley Eder' of the 'Detroit Free Press,' Detroit, Michigan.

Shirley dear,

Thank you for your article of October 6. I've just returned from Washington. D.C after a five day 'Joan Crawford Film Festival' at the American Film Institute and a day of autographing my new book at Woodward & Lothrop. Then I went to San Francisco and Los Angeles. The tour is going great guns. Now I have thirteen more cities to do (for you know what soft drink) and the book.

- Much, much love - Joan.

February 16, 1972.

Dear Dollee,

Thank you so much for the lovely Christmas card and your very kind personal handwritten message. I was so pleased that you thought of me at Christmas time. Yes, my address is still 8008 West Norton Ave., Los Angeles, Calif. 90046.

My congratulations to you and your husband upon being grandparents of twin girls. From now on, I'm sure your lives will have a happier, fuller meaning. Yes, I do have twin daughters. They are married now, incidentally: and Cathy has a daughter and Cindy has two sons. Bless you, and every good wish to you for a wonderfully happy and healthful New Year.

- Joan Crawford.

November 27, 1972 - To Mrs. Frances Spingold.

Frances, dear heart -

I, too, am sad you went off to Palm Beach before I could visit you here and say goodbye. You were always happier in Palm Beach than in New York and I'm happy for you as I feel you will relax more there.

*How nice that you have a wonderful nurse and I hope your new couple is working out and taking good care of your comforts and needs. Thank Mr. Stephenson (*her secretary*) for his kind thoughts and to you, my beloved friend Frances, all my love and tender friendship.*

- Always, Joan.

May 7, 1973 - A handwritten recipe for "Baked Ham" on "From the desk of Joan Crawford" imprinted stationary -

1 can of Dole pineapple chunks (large)
Pour juice around base of ham, cloves all over it. Spread mustard over it.
Roll brown sugar and sprinkle over it - also cinnamon.
Pineapple chunks, (toothpick in each one). I cup of water, just in base of ham.
Pre-heat oven @ 325 F for 1 hour. Cook ham @ 325 F for 1 hour.
(Sprinkle sugar in juice & water after 1/2 hour of cooking).

July 16, 1973.

Dear Joseph Cohen,
Thank you for your very nice letter telling me about the celebrity auction you planned to hold. I am sorry for this delay in answering, but your letter was sent to me on West North Avenue, and I live on West Norton Avenue, and it was just forwarded to me.
I am enclosing one of my monogrammed handkerchiefs that you may sell at the auction, although I realize that I may be late in getting this little gift to you. All good wishes to you, and I hope the event will be wonderfully successful.
- Joan Crawford.

February 20, 1974 ~ To author, 'Lawrence J. Quirk.'

Larry Dear,
Thank you for your good letter of the eleventh, and the cover of your new book, 'The Great Romantic Films' - and what an impressive cover it is! And thank you - I feel very complimented that I am on the cover, Larry dear.
I didn't see Michael Moriarty in 'Find Your Way Home', but did see him in Katharine Hepburn's, 'The Glass Menagerie' on television, and I thought he was brilliant. Yes, William Haines' death was a great shock to me, but he suffered for many months, so I know it was a blessing. He was a rare and wonderful friend. I miss him very much. God bless and my love, as ever...
- Joan.

William Haines was one of Joan's loyalist and lifelong friends. A major star in his own right he joined MGM in the early 1920's and he quickly became one of the few stars who earned the right to have their name *above* the opening title of a film. He starred in MGM's first talkie and was a regular in the popularity polls as one of the studios most desirable leading men, but alas, it wasn't to last.

William Haines, commonly known as 'Billy,' fell in love with his stand in, Jimmy Shields and by 1923, they were living together as a couple. In a time where actor's morals were highly regarded, Louis B. Mayer, did everything in his power to cover up his leading man's homosexuality.

It was not uncommon for gay stars to marry, in order to portray a 'clean' public image, just so long as they hid what they did when behind closed doors, marriages of convenience were common place.

Still on the rise herself, and a close friend of Billy, Joan Crawford pitched him a deal. *"Let's get married, Billy,"* she proposed. She knew it was for show, but she didn't care. It helped Billy and it helped her. Billy didn't share her enthusiasm, and as much as he loved Joan, he refused her proposal without a second thought. He loved Jimmy, and that was that.

Louis B. Mayer was furious at Billy's refusal to play along with the studios policy of either being a serial dater or happily married man so he gave him an ultimatum. It was his lifestyle or his career. Once again, Billy didn't give it a second thought. He chose love, he chose Jimmy.
Mayer ripped up his contract and vowed that he'd make sure that he'd never work in the movie business again!

In a way he was right. Billy Haines never worked in front of the cameras again but he did have an active role in Hollywood, for many, many years. He and Jimmy Shields opened an antique shop in 1930, slowly moving across into interior design and into the homes of every well-known Hollywood celebrity of their time. Their star clients included, Lionel Barrymore, Claudette Colbert, Marion Davies, Bette Davis, George Cukor, Carole Lombard, Jack Warner, and of course, Joan Crawford.

Billy Haines died of cancer in 1973. Just three months later, his lover of fifty years, took his own life, in order to be with him for eternity. Joan Crawford was once quoted as saying, *"The happiest marriage I've seen in Hollywood is Billy Haines and Jimmy Shields."*

March 1st, 1974 - To gossip columnist, 'Shirley Eder' of the 'Detroit Free Press.'

Shirley darling,
Thank you very much for your note and your new address and telephone number. Since when am I in a '69th Street fortress?" - If it is, it is a lovely one. With the moving and my work for Pepsi, I have not had time to read your book, 'Not This Time, Cary Grant' - I don't like to start

*a book and pick it up again one week later, so I will read it in one sitting
very soon. Much, much love, dear friend.*

- Joan.

June 20, 1975.

Harry Dear,

*Please forgive this very tardy letter to thank you and the National
Association of Greeting Card Publishers for naming me, 'Mother of the
year 1975' but I've been traveling for Pepsi. I'm so deeply grateful to all
of you for the great honor you have bestowed upon me. My children are so
very proud, and so am I.*

*Thank you, too, for your note yesterday and the enclosed article
on Brad. You, too, have a wonderful reason to be proud. I would so love to
see you, your wife and Brad again sometime soon. Bless you my dear
friend, and please have a glorious summer.*

- Much affection, always, Joan.

Carl Johnes, author of, *Crawford: The Last Years*, had a close
friendship with Joan during the last decade of her life. In his book, he
writes about a phone conversation that he was having with Joan, when
suddenly he had to cut the conversation short because his dog, Augusta,
needed her nightly walk in the park.

"I hope you have a nice warm coat for her to wear," Joan asked.

Johnes sighed, and repeated what he'd told her many times before,
*"Joan, Augusta is not a fancy little movie-star dog. She's a sturdy little
hound who -"*

Before he could finish, Joan cut him off, *"Honey, please! - You
mean to tell me she has nothing to wear?"*

"No," answered, Johnes.

*"I will not allow you to take that dog outside when it is five below
zero,"* Joan scolded. *"Now, just do me a favor; take a tape measure and
figure out the distance between the back of her neck and where her tail
starts, and call me back."*

Johnes did as he was told, and within two weeks a package arrived
at his door addressed to *"Miss Augusta Johnes, c/o Carl Johnes,"* with a
note wishing her a *"Merry Christmas from Princess"* (Joan's Shih Tzu).
According to Johnes, Augusta looked great in her new outfit, but she hated
wearing it. He did manage to keep it on her long enough to snap a Polaroid
for Joan. He sent the picture along with this note, *"My person tells me that
your person is a famous movie star. Although I only know Lassie, Benji
and Morris the cat, I am sure this "Joan Crawford" is a very nice person
to have."* Joan was thrilled with the photo and cleverly written note, but

she never found out that Augusta continued her nightly walks in the park, *without* clothes.

October 5, 1976.

Mary dear,

 Thank you for your very sweet letters and the lovely greeting cards. You are always so thoughtful. I'm delighted you enjoyed seeing Christina on Merv Griffin's Show. I thought she looked lovely too, and I am very proud of her.

 No, I didn't buy a cabin cruiser. I can't imagine where that rumor ever started, I've never even thought about buying a boat. I've spent most of the summer traveling in Europe on business trips so it is good to be home again. Bless you and have a happy fall season.

          - As ever, Joan.

No date - 1977 - To 'George Cukor' - Probably a thank you note for a birthday present, her last.

My very dear George,

 You do find the most divine gifts The large box of bitter mints are heaven, and from London yet! Thank you so very much for thinking of me so generously at this special time of the year. I saw a picture of you in a magazine recently and you look sensational, which makes me very happy.

      - Constant love from your devoted - Joan.

April 5, 1977.

My dear Barbara,

 Thank you for your sweet letter and the lovely birthday card. It was dear of you to remember my special day, and I am very grateful to you. I am so sorry to hear about your husband, I can well understand that you miss him very much. The period of adjustment can be very difficult, I know. The only advice I can give you is to keep active.

 After my husband passed away, I did a great deal of charitable work for national charities, and I found that very helpful, as I felt I was helping others. Bless you - and please know that my thoughts are with you.

          - Joan Crawford

 A little over a month after the above letter was written, On May 10th, 1977, Joan Crawford passed away. Joan Crawford *was* Hollywood, and Hollywood, as we knew it, died right along with her.

Famous Friends

"Nobody can imitate me. You can always see impersonations of Katharine Hepburn and Marilyn Monroe. But not me. Because I've always drawn on myself only."

- Joan Crawford.

The following collections of letters were written *to* Joan Crawford from other celebrities and movie stars. Some are in response to a note that she'd obviously written to them, others are congratulatory letters for her Best Actress Academy Award of 1946 for, *Mildred Pierce.*

Incidentally, Joan's beloved Best Actress Oscar was put up for public auction after her death. The 1993 auction was still a few years before the lucrative movie memorabilia market had peaked and it's estimated catalog value of $15,000, jumped to a final sell price of $68,000. This seemingly inflated price raised eyebrows at the time of sale, but in comparison to today's prices, it was an absolute steal!

The first Academy Awards presentation took place on 16 May, 1929, it honored the best film work produced between August 1927 thru July 1928. MGM art director, Cedric Gibbons, designed the statue of a man with a crusader's sword standing on a reel of film. At 13 1/2 inches tall, and plated in 24 carat gold, Oscar's value is a mere $250 USD. Of course, monetarily, at least to a recipient's career, the value of winning this prestigious statue can mean a pay rise of millions and a permanent place in Hollywood history.

Any Academy Award given out before the 1950's can openly be sold at auction, but in order to protect the significance of the award, AMPAS (Academy of Motion Picture Arts and Science) has made it a rule, that any recipient from the 1950's to the present must sell the award back to the Academy only. The winner must sign this agreement before taking the award home.

Any thoughts of selling the Oscar to AMPAS for a comparable price that they'd get on the open market is also squashed, the Award will be bought back by AMPAS, at the bargain price of $1!

Of course, some of the most historically significant Oscars were given out before this rule came into effect, hence the industry buzz when they do hit the auction block. The 1938 Best Actress Oscar that Bette Davis won for *Jezebel* was auctioned by Christies in 2001. The final price paid by an anonymous telephone bidder was a staggering, $578,000!

It was later discovered, that anonymous phone bid was placed by Steven Spielberg, not for himself, but for the Academy of Motion Picture Arts and Sciences. It was to be a donation, and a not too shabby tax write off to boot!

Clark Gable's Oscar for his performance in the 1934 classic, *It Happened One Night* has the honor of being the second highest amount paid for an award. The new owner wrote a check for $607,000. Once again, it was Steven Spielberg who bought the statue and once again he kindly donated it back to the Academy.

In a letter to the Academy, Spielberg gave his reasons for his purchase and subsequent donation: *The Oscar Statuette is the most personal recognition of good work our industry can ever bestow, and it strikes me as a sad sign of our times that this icon could be confused with a commercial treasure.*

Still, this exorbitant amount isn't the highest price ever paid for an Oscar. That title goes to the Best Picture Oscar awarded to David O. Selznick for *Gone With The Wind* - The bidder? No, not Steven Spielberg. It was the one and only Michael Jackson. The price? A staggering, $1.54 million! The difference between Michael Jackson and Steven Spielberg? Michael Jackson kept it! Spielberg did manage to pick up a treasure for himself that day, he paid $220,000 for Clark Gable's personal script from, *Gone With The Wind.* An item he intends to keep in his personal collection.

It's interesting to note the human connection between those few individual Oscars put up for sale on the secondary market. Of course, Joan Crawford and Bette Davis had one of Hollywood's longest and most notorious rivalries, while on the other hand, Clark Gable and Joan Crawford had one of Hollywood's longest and most notorious love affairs.

The most affordable personal Oscar to go up for auction was in 1988. For the bargain price of $13,500, someone other than Marlon Brando bought the privilege of owning his Best Actor Oscar for his role in *On The Waterfront.* On the other end of the financial scale, Vivien Leigh's *Gone With The Wind* Oscar sold for a staggering $563,000!

A great deal of the paraphrased letters within this chapter cover Joan's nomination and subsequent Oscar win, whilst others are written at various times and events throughout her life. Whatever the subject matter, these letters were written by some of the most powerful people in Hollywood history. It's an interesting insight into the circle of friends and peers who felt the need to send their congratulations to the Best Actress of 1946 - Joan Crawford..........their friend.

July, 2, 1941 - A letter written by Jill Esmond to her son, Tarquin Olivier. Jill Esmond was once the wife of Laurence Olivier and Tarquin was their son - In part.

...Her adopted daughter is charming and Joan is very sweet with her. Joan had just got her adopted son, about seven weeks old. I gave him his bottle and it was lovely to hold a very tiny baby again. I wonder if she will get fed up with them.

Tarquin comments: *"As neighbors of Joan Crawford we knew none of this child abuse. My recollection is of a goody two-shoes atmosphere, all pretend and prissy, like the plastic covers on their chintz cushions."*

February 4, 1946 - Typed letter on personal letterhead from Helen Hayes congratulating Joan on her nomination for Best Actress of 1946. She says, *"Darling, I'm so happy and as proud as if I had given birth to you."* She goes on to say that she realizes that it's bad luck to assume she's going to win the prestigious award, but she knows that *"her Joan"* and Oscar are already joined. She praises Joan's performance in the film, telling her she caught a showing of the film two nights ago and she thought she was *"superb"* in it.

It's apparent that Helen Hayes and Joan Crawford had a solid and long-standing friendship. Proof of which is this letter's existence in 1946, and another shorter letter that's quoted further in, dated twenty-six years later, in 1972.

Still, as close as they were as friends, Helen Hayes had an insiders view of Joan Crawford/Mother and she wasn't shy in expressing her view of what she saw. She was once quoted as saying, *"You know, the one thing Joan should not have been is a mother. She couldn't do that role very well. But as an actress and as a person, as a friend, (she had) people who adore her."*

March 8, 1946. - On 'Hal B. Wallis' letterhead. He congratulates her on her Oscar win and regrets that she wasn't in attendance to accept the award in person. He tells her she was a very popular win and her statue is well deserved. He signs his letter, *"sincerely, Hal."*

March 8, 1946 - On 'Sam Jaffe' letterhead. He sends his best wishes for her speedy recovery and congratulates her on her win. He foresees her doing many more *"good pictures"* like *Mildred Pierce* and

171

hopes they'll produce even more Oscars for her. He signs, *"sincerest best wishes, Sam."*

No date, but the content of this letter is yet another congratulatory note on Joan's Best Actress win for, *Mildred Pierce*. Written on La Quinta Hotel stationary letterhead, from fellow actress, Irene Dunne. She tells Joan that she knows Mr. Curtiz is jumping with joy at the news of her win. She said she can't wait to work with him (Curtiz) in her next picture and goes on to wish her many more triumphs in the years to come. She signs, *"sincerely, Irene Dunne."*

March 8, 1946 - A handwritten letter on personal letterhead from 'Barbara Stanwyck.' In a somewhat short note from Joan's close friend, Barbara sends Joan her congratulations and regrets that she was not there to accept her award in person. She wishes her even greater success in the future before signing off as, *"Barbara."*

March 8, 1946 - Typed congratulatory letter on 'H.M.Warner' letterhead. Mr. Warner writes on behalf of he and his wife, sending Joan their warmest wishes and telling her there is no news in the world that could have made them happier. He ends with, *"you see, hard work and sincere effort pays off."* - He signs, *"sincerely, Harry."*

March 8, 1946 - Typed letter signed Jack (Warner) on 'Warner Bros' letterhead. Jack Warner starts off by telling Joan how sorry he was that she was too sick to attend the Oscar ceremony and accept her award in person. He praises her *"grand performance"* in *Mildred Pierce* and expresses his personal pride and the pride of the entire studio for her win. He asks that they can arrange to get together as soon as possible before informally signing off as, *"Jack."*

No date, 1946 - A handwritten congratulatory letter from 'Billie Burke' on winning the Oscar for *Mildred Pierce*. A warm letter of congratulations from Billie Burke, at first apologizing for bothering her amidst the joy of her excitement at winning the *"cherished prize."* She recalls the day in Mr. Curtiz' office when he spoke of his wish to see Joan win the Best Actress Award and she expresses her overwhelming joy that his wish, and hers eventually came true. She signs off as, *"Billie."*

A very animated, humorous handwritten note, undated, from Noel Coward, expressing the realization that a thought just popped into his head that he has loved *"his Joanie"* for thirty-nine years! - He calls it a *"rush of emotion"* that he thought she needed to hear and signs the note, *"Noelie."*

From Peter Ustinov - undated. In response to a note that Joan has written to him, congratulating him on his Emmy win, Ustinov tells her he will keep her note amongst his most treasured possessions. He ends his letter by telling her that he hopes he has given her a mere fraction of the pleasure that she has given to him. He signs, *"love Peter."*

Because this is an undated letter, I can only estimate its 'possible date' by the information provided in its content. Peter Ustinov won his first Emmy Award in 1958, for 'Best Single Performance - Lead or Support', in *Omnibus* - Episode: *The Life of Samuel Johnson.*

His second award was in 1967, again for 'Best Single Performance - Lead or Support,' in *Barefoot In Athens*, a made for television movie. His third win was in 1970, again it was in the category of 'Best Single Performance - Lead or Support,' in *Storm in Summer*, yet another made for television movie. This places his letter within a twelve-year time frame, so for that reason, I have placed it in the middle of that period of correspondence.

March 13th, 1946 - From ex-mother in law - 'Mary Pickford.' She tells her former daughter in law that she was unable to attend the ceremony the night before but they were all clustered around the radio listening for the results. She excitedly tells Joan that a collective *"whoop"* went up when her name was announced and tells her she knows the whole industry was rooting for her to win. Still, she assures her there were greater rooters than the group at Pickfair. She signs, *"as ever, affectionately yours, Mary Pickford."*

March 16, 1946 - On 'Paramount Pictures Inc' letterhead. In a brief note, Charles Brackett and Billy Wilder send their collective good wishes on Joan's Oscar win by at first expressing their concern over the flu that kept her away from the ceremony and secondly telling her that the night was a circus and she was the Queen. They end with, *"we love you always, Charles and Billy."*

April 20, 1959 - From Dinah Shore and George Montgomery, just one day after the death of Joan's fourth husband, Al Steele. A loving and sympathetic note from the couple expressing their deep sorrow on Al's passing. She tells Joan of her feelings of helplessness in easing her grief but assures her that whatever little comfort they can bring to her in any way, with anything at all, don't hesitate to ask them and they will be there. *"You are not alone in your sorrow, dear friend,"* she says, before signing off, *"all our love, always Dinah and George."*

November 1, 1965 on 'Alfred Hitchcock' personal letterhead and signed, *'Hitch."* A humorous note from the master of suspense, he addresses her as *"my dear Joan,"* before telling her that in one of his rare homosexual moments when he finds himself flicking through the pages of Vogue, he came across a magnificent photo of her and he felt compelled to compliment her on it. He signs, *"sincerely, Hitch."*

April 14, 1966 - A typed letter on personal letterhead from ex-mother-in law, Mary Pickford. A thank you note of sorts, since Pickford compliments Joan in the first paragraph by telling her that her heart is very large and loving. She says, *"no wonder you have so many staunch friends."* In reflection she tells Joan that time is passing quickly and she regrets they don't have a chance to see more of each other. She tells Joan that Lillian Gish is staying with her and calls her a *"darling little work horse, the spirit of eternal youth."* She says that while she greatly admires both Joan's and Lillian's work ethic, she is content to sit back and hold her hand over her fat tummy and enjoy retirement. She signs off, *"with fond affection of many years gone by, your mother in law, Mamma Ullman, twice removed, Mary."*

March 8th, no year - On Larry King Letterhead paper. A handwritten letter by talk show guru Larry King. He starts off by thanking Joan for her lovely letter in which he will treasure always. He says it was his absolute honor to have interviewed her and happily tells her that the show she appeared on received a great reaction. He ends with, *"I am now a confirmed Pepsi drinker. Love Larry."*

No date, no place - a handwritten thank you letter to Joan from Liza Minnelli. The letter thanks her for the lovely evening and the *"surprise."* She gushes about the food they ate at Cafe Brasilia and of how well she thought Joan looked that evening. Liza tells Joan that she hopes Pepsi appreciate her invaluable contribution to the company and ends with *"love and gratitude, Liza."*

July 31, 1966, a handwritten letter from Henry Fonda telling Joan that of course he understands her not being able to attend their party. He says she was missed, but they're both glad that Cindy is now okay. He signs, *"love Hank."*

April 22, 1969 - On *Cactus Flower* letterhead. A handwritten letter from Ingrid Bergman. Underneath the date she has written, *"On the set of 'Walk in the Spring Rain,'"* most likely a working title for the film, later released as *Cactus Flower.*

She thanks Joan for her wire of good wishes and tells her how happy she is to have finally started work on the film. She asks after Joan's children and tells her that she has a brief visit from her children over the Easter vacation. Her only regret is that her pictures are being shot so close together, as it gives her no time to return home to her family. She signs, *"all my warmest wishes, Ingrid."*

July 6, 1971 - A typed letter from 'Noel Coward' on 'Les Avants sur Montreux' letterhead. He starts off with, *"Joan Darling,"* and begins by thanking her for her sweet note about his film, *The Astonished Heart.* He tells her that it was not well received upon its initial release but subsequent TV showings have given it a new lease on life, which for him is very gratifying.

He tells her to thank Princess (Joan's Shih Tzu) for the lovely photo and to kiss her for him. He tells her that she will take pride of place in his photograph album, entitled, "Noel Coward and Friends." He ends with, *"my dear love, as always and again, my thanks darling, Noel."*

December 23, 1971 - A handwritten letter on personal letterhead and signed with Barbara Stanwyck's nickname, *'Missy.'* She thanks Joan for the lovely plant and words of good cheer during her recent illness. She signs, *"happy days for you my dear friend, love Missy."*

January 27, 1972 - On 'John Huston' letterhead. He begins his letter by telling Joan what a wonderfully thoughtful person she is. He tells her that he's been speaking about her to John Foreman, a producer on his last picture and he told him a delightful story about her that he'd like to relay to her. He said that when John Forman was a young agent with the MCA office, he and two other agents would take you to the theater. He said it was quite a site as the three of them would play musical chairs for the privilege of sitting next to you.

He asks if she'll be coming to California any time soon and remembers the last time he saw her was at a German lawn party, of all things. He tells her if he has to go to another one of those events to see her, he will, although he'd much prefer her to come to California instead! He signs, *"as ever, John."*

March 8, 1972, from David Niven, a week after his 62nd Birthday. He begins with, *"Darling Joan,"* and starts by thanking her for his birthday telegramme and review about his new book. He ends with, *"I never shall forget your sweetness in my darkest hour, best love, David."*

An interesting letter to Joan from David Niven. The book he mentioned was, *The Moon's a Balloon.* His 'darkest hour' was his reference to the tragic death of his wife, Primula Rollo.

Married for just six years, and having two young sons, David Jr. and Jamie, 28 year old Primula died after falling down some basement steps at a party in Tyrone Power's home.

The night of the accident, Joan offered to take in the two young Niven boys to save them from the trauma of spending the night at the hospital. Unfortunately, the fractured skull and brain lacerations that Primula received from the fall, caused her untimely death the following day.

Although he eventually remarried and had two daughters with, Hjordis Tersmeden, friends have often said the six years of marriage he shared with 'Primmie' were the happiest of his life. David Niven died in 1983, he was 73.

March 16, 1972 - From, *'James Cagney.'* He begins by thanking her for her sweet note and goes on to tell her about the pact that he and Spencer Tracy made thirty years ago about never traveling abroad until they were washed up in the picture business. He tells her the main reason for the decision was that there was simply no comfort in traveling because the press followed them everywhere.

He says, *"then came TV and that really kept us home!"* He sadly states that he only wishes Spence could have hung in a little longer to enjoy the fruits of his labor. He ends with a line that you can almost hear him saying, *" all for now, girl, love from me, Jim C."*

October 6, 1972 - On 'George Cukor' personal letterhead, regarding a George Cukor - Joan Crawford retrospective, signed, *"George."* He tells Joan that it's ridiculous to think that his name would ever take first billing over *"the* Joan Crawford*"* and he wishes she could have taken the stage with him to make their bows together. He tells her there's a second chance for both of them since the show was so popular, it'll run again in Washington. He asks that she try to make that one so they can take their bows, together, as it should be.

August 8, no year, from, 'Michael Learned' aka Olivia Walton of, *The Waltons,* television show. She tells Joan that she was so excited to receive a letter from her that she jumped all over the living room. She tells Joan that she has always admired her, not only as an actress, but also as a woman. She ends with, *"warmest regards, Michael Learned."*

January 18th, no year - From 'Ellen Corby', Grandma Walton on *The Waltons*. Probably a 1970's letter since a newspaper article enclosed with the letter mentions the television shows, *'M*A*S*H* and *Police Woman*, two top rated television shows of this period.

She starts with, *"Dearest Joan,"* and tells her how wonderful it was to hear her voice on the phone again, she says, *"you sounded as vivacious as ever!"* She ends with, *"love you, Ellen."*

There was a newspaper snippet enclosed with this letter with a quote from Ellen Corby about Joan - It reads: *'I worked with Joan Crawford on five films, and I've never met anyone who was more dedicated...an absolute perfectionist and a warm human being, too.'* She added this footnote in her own hand underneath the article, *"I said much more but they condensed it down to this - Love, Ellen."*

August 24, 1973 - From George Cukor, on personal letterhead. He starts with, *"My dear Joan,"* and reminisces about their time together in old Hollywood by recalling how they used to have to time a kiss with a stop watch, or how he used to have to check her décolletage within a sixteenth of an inch, and perhaps the most frustrating, the scenes when a husband and wife were in their nuptial bed, it would only be approved by the sensors if one of them had one foot on the floor! He says the thought, or even the idea of a non-husband and wife in a non-nuptial bed - *"heaven forbid!"*

He makes the somewhat prudish comparisons of yesteryear to the loose morals of the seventies by saying there is no limit to what is seen these days, it's all about making a *"fast buck."* He says the part that saddens him the most is that the big family audiences have been alienated by this new form of filmmaking. He even goes as far as to blame President Nixon by saying all this filth only came about when he and his *"sanctimonious, hollier than thou hypocrites were running things!"*

He tells Joan that he feels that Louis B. Mayer only ever put up with him because *"he was never particularly nice to me."* He says that Mayer's daughters told him that their father's beliefs were that pictures were for families and the moment that theory is abandoned, disaster would strike. He goes on to say that *"Louis (although I never dared call him that)"* had outward morals as high as the sky, but his personal carryings on, such as Ginny Sims, Ann Miller, Hedy Lamarr and on and on, were simply not talked about.

He ends with, *"as for nudity, there was infinitely more eroticism generated by ladies like you, fully clothed! - Always, George."*

January 4, 1974 - On 'Douglas Fairbanks Jr. Letterhead.' A loving letter from Joan's ex-husband. It is somewhat interesting to see that he still refers to her as, *'Billie.'* He starts with, *"Billie Dear,"* and blames his constant state of jet lag for his forgetfulness in thanking her for his lovely birthday and Christmas messages. He says, both greetings are very much appreciated, although he's beginning to wish there was no such occasion as birthdays anymore! He ends with, *"love, Doug,"* but adds a particularly cute postscript, saying, *"I sat through 'Our Dancing Daughters' on T.V. the other night and it was, and you were enchanting! - Isn't it funny how, "Tempess" does "Fugit?"*

April 25, 1975 - Handwritten note from 'Loretta Young, 'signed, *'Gretch.'* In part she tells Joan, *"you forget, we were all beautiful then, and in all honesty, I don't think we appreciated it at all. It takes so long to mature, to understand the true values of life."*

Some forty years prior to this letter being written, Loretta Young, known for her 'goody-goody' attitudes, did her best to avoid a drunken Joan at a 1930's Hollywood cocktail party. Joan only ever saw her avoidance as a snub and stopped George Cukor sitting on the couch next to her by remarking, 'You can't sit there, that's Loretta Young's chair - you can tell by the cross mark on the seat!'

June 30, 1975 - Handwritten letter on 'Barbara Stanwyck' personal letterhead, signed, *'Missy.'* In part she tells Joan that her photograph has been removed from her house and she believes the culprit is the day maid. She asks Joan for a replacement and signs off, *"love, Missy."*

Ironically the only two photos that were on display in Joan Crawford's apartment at the time of her death, were of the late President, John F. Kennedy and her friend of many decades, Barbara Stanwyck.

January 21, 1976 - On George Cukor Letterhead Paper. A particularly touching letter, with recognition of Joan's promptness in writing a thank you note. He starts by saying his head is bowed in shame, *"oh why couldn't I have taken a leaf out of Joan Crawford's book of Beautiful Behavior, sat right down and written a thank you note?"* He said he's so grateful to have all the lovely new napkins, and in all shapes and sizes. He tells Joan that he knows his guests will be dazzled with them for a long time and when he's complimented on them he'll brag that they were a gift from *"my darling friend, Joan."*

He says he does have a small excuse for being so tardy in his reply, he's been looping, dubbing and winding up the picture, *The Blue Bird* and he will *"try its wings"* sometime in the spring, probably in Washington. He signs, *"always, George."*

The Blue Bird, starred Elizabeth Taylor, Jane Fonda, Ava Gardner, Cicely Tyson and Robert Morley, however despite this all-star cast, not even the talents of George Cukor could make this movie work. It succumbed to scathing reviews and in his third last stint as Director, George Cukor (he was 76 years old at the time) suffered the cliché sad end to an illustrious career by continuing to work, way past his prime.

April 6, 1976 - On 'Samuel Goldwyn, Jr.' letterhead he thanks Joan for her wishes of sympathy on the death of his beloved mother. He agrees with her that she was indeed a beautiful and vital lady and he tells her he knows he was lucky to have her as a mother for as long as he did. He tells Joan that his mother had great admiration for her and because of that, her note of sympathy holds a particularly special meaning for him. He signs, *"sincerely, Sam."*

In an issue of 'Hollywood Magazine' of January 1941, an open letter from Joan Crawford was published in response to the scathing attack that Ed Sullivan wrote about her in his syndicated column. Ed Sullivan's Newspaper Column, published on October 6th, 1940 stated the following: He starts off by saying that it's about time to *"crack down on wide-eyed Joan Crawford."* He says for many years he's sincerely tried to like her, but she so often strains the point of friendship that something has to give, and this time, it GAVE! He says there is no one performer who exclaims that that press of the country is unfair with her and he continues his tongue lashing by saying, *"I don't know anyone who has gone so far in this business with so little talent as La Crawford."*

He goes on to attack her latest picture, *Susan and God*, by saying that it was a flop because firstly, the part was entirely unsuited to her talent and secondly and perhaps more importantly, *"her contract with the public has been broken."*

He closes by saying that no longer will he rush to her defense when other movie stars put the *"blast on her"* for her insincerity, or for her *"affections."*

Joan Crawford's open letter to Ed Sullivan - 'Hollywood Magazine' - January, 1941, in response to his scathing public attack in his column.

Dear Ed Sullivan,

Goodness knows I do often rap people and I'm honest enough to admit it, although I'm not proud of myself for doing so. Naturally, when I read your blast in the paper, my first emotion was to wish you boiled in oil. Then I thought: 'No, it's over and done with. Let it pass. Forget it.'

But this view, I concluded in time, was wrong. It implied submissiveness. Hence this letter, meant not so much to slap back at you as to take a definite stand on this business of 'cooperation', to inquire, perhaps, what it means and set you right on a point or two.

You say that for some years you have tried to like me. Ed, how? By seeing me? By talking to me - as friends? No indeed. I haven't seen you since I separated from Franchot. And before that I talked to you exactly twice, once when I was in New York as a visiting fireman - when I asked to see you. You had printed something perfectly silly and I thought it could be straightened out if we talked it over like civilized people. Besides, I thought it high time we met. I remember that you were kind enough to invite Franchot and me to dine with you and your very attractive wife.
Those were the only times I've ever seen you. And for the life of me, I cannot remember any great effort you made to know and like me.

I have never 'exclaimed that the press of the country has been unfair' to me. I have said, however, that a columnist - any columnist - is unfair to attack anyone who has no means of reply. (This does not include legitimate criticism of commercial entertainment or art by properly qualified critics.) Certainly, I have complained about that. Not for myself alone but for my craft and everyone so attacked. I consider it cheap, tawdry, and gangster journalism. I have never ceased to marvel at the paradox or otherwise respectable newspapers that are serving their community constructively and who, at the same time, permit journalistic lice to stink up their pages. If you so desire, I will tell you that at 42nd Street and Broadway through a loudspeaker.

'While she has been in the East, Miss Crawford was asked by two newspapers to cooperate with them in stunts which would have placed her in a favorable light,' you say. Ed, publicized acts of mine are not premeditated, nor for the purpose of placing me in a favorable light with newspapers or the public. Goodness knows, certainly I do, that a motion picture actress without a public would be a thing of beauty, perhaps, and a cipher forever. That much is true. But how in the name of heaven does she

179

acquire that public? Because she fell out of a tree into the arms of a movie scout? Or because Darryl Zanuck happened to see a picture of her in a cigarette advertisement? Or because she did some occasional hoofing for the Schuberts?

What this last might explain is merely how she gets into pictures. - not how she acquires a public. This public she acquires, if she does, by hard work. But the press, you shriek! - Yes, indeed, the papers helped. And the magazines, too. And she is properly grateful. And how does she show it? By doing everything from lolling around in pajamas to jumping through a hoop, for the benefit of a photographer. For years she does all that. Comes an occasion when she does not leap through the hoop. Then annihilation! But - supposing we turn to your column:

'On both occasions she delegated the task of breaking bad news, her refusal, to MGM publicity men. In other words, Joan didn't have the nerve or the courtesy to call the newspapermen or their offices to say no,' you lash out. Since the invitation to appear at the Daily News Harvest Moon Ball came from MGM publicity men, it is perfectly natural that the refusal went to them. I even explained that I was in the country with my infant child who was ill with a cold. And whether you like it or not, Ed, I would not have left her for any favorable publicity.

The other affront to a paper, if I must go into weary detail, was perpetrated with even greater innocence on my part. Too late for any possible cancellation of plans, I received a vague and belated request to cooperate in a fashion show staged by the Chicago Tribune, for which paper I have nothing but respect. The show would have been underway and over by the time I managed to straighten out my affairs and fly down to Chicago.

Your comment on the box-office results of 'Susan and God' places you in the position of having information not available to me. However, if you are interested in accuracy you can probably get the correct information from MGM - and according to Mr. Mayer last week, 'Susan', was doing all right.

Here's another little gem of yours:' I don't know really anyone who has gone so far in this business with so little talent as La Crawford.' Aw, Ed, how could you? As long as I was getting away with murder, why turn stool pigeon and snitch on me? When one is blessed with such magnificent talents as you are, Ed, you must try to be more patient with the less fortunate, non-talented Crawfords.

Your petulant, 'I confess that I've lost patience with Joan Crawford', is Age II stuff. Please, Mr. Dictator, don't banish me because I have lost favor with you.' No longer will this pillar rush to her defense when other movie stars put the blast on her for her insincerity or her affectations,' you write.

Any time you 'rush to my defense', it has been because of your own free will. I have never asked you to do so. The times I have seen you and had occasion to talk to you it has been as a friend to whom I desired to give my side of a story in detail. To hell with whether you retracted anything or not. It was you as a person that I wanted to be fair. My batting average with respect to requests from your paper, The Daily News, has been pretty good. Last April I accepted an invitation and attended a cocktail party given by the News during the publishers' convention. I considered it an honor and a friendly act to be invited. By the same token I considered the invitation to the Harvest Moon Ball as an honor. and a friendly act. It was simply impossible for me to attend.

And as for not answering the telephone (as Tyrone Power and Annabella presumable do) what with a 'secretary' guarding me from callers, please be informed that the only time I don't happen to pick up a telephone is when my maid - I don't even have a secretary - beats me to it.

From here on your column trails off into a welter of abuse, bearing little or no connection with the subject at hand. You take time off to compare me to George Raft, 'a nice guy', who makes the nightclubs and does the right thing. I, too, regard George Raft as a 'nice guy', just as free to attend nightclubs and opening nights at the bistros as I fee free to pass them up, possibly because I don't seem to enjoy these affairs quite so much as Mr. Raft does. Then, too, I don't happen to be financially interested in nightclubs as is Mr. Raft.

What I have been trying to say is that what columning needs, apparently is not the only 'divine dispassion' supposedly the very soul of a good reporter, not only the sense of fair play, not only a disposition to remain always selfless and to make a religion of facts, but, above all, a recollection that an actress, even one who makes bad pictures, is an actress first, and a trained seal secondly. So that possibly she may be forgiven when she stumbles. Okay, Ed?

- Sincerely, Joan Crawford

The Art of Graphonalysis

"Oh dear, who was she?"
        - Joan Crawford on hearing that Pearl Harbor was gone.

In gathering Joan's letters for this book, I came to realize that many of her early letters were handwritten. As the years progressed, she took to typing most of her correspondence, however she would still put pen to paper for close friends, on occasion. During the hours it took to decipher these handwritten letters, I saw the development of her handwriting, and thought it would be interesting to find out what Joan's handwriting said about her.

Because the brain controls the hand, it is virtually impossible to change your style of writing to cheat your way into a better reading. Besides, when Joan was writing her letters, she was writing, from her heart, from her head, it was her writing in its raw state, no acting via the written word at all.   In reality, a Graphonalysis report of Joan's handwriting would be one of the most honest evaluations of who she really was, as a person.

Handwriting analysis, or Graphonalysis, (as it's technically known), is the study of a persons handwriting characteristics to determine their overall personality. It isn't a psychic reading; it's an exact science. It is so well respected, that many corporations now use certified Graphologist's to determine who would be the best employee for a new job position or company promotion. Handwriting analysis is also commonly used in criminal cases; it can even help you find the perfect life partner!

A lot of factors determine the final results. The brush strokes, spacing between words, pressure of the pen to paper, size of the writing are all studied closely. As a result of that study, the personality of any given individual can be easily revealed. However, in Joan's case, there was one small problem. I couldn't possibly hand over a selection of Joan's letters and tell the Graphologist, who wrote them. Joan Crawford's celebrity image would have to color her report. There was absolutely no way she could stay impartial after knowing she was analyzing Joan Crawford's handwriting. So, I went to painstaking lengths to block out Joan's name on the letterhead paper, blacken her signature, and only give the expert a selection of letters that made no mention of famous names or movies that may connect the letters to Joan.

LaVina Pratt, a qualified handwriting expert, highly respected in her field, willingly agreed to this experiment. LaVina graduated from the International Graphoanalysis Institute in 1977, going on to obtain her Masters Degree in the field, in 1994. She travels the world, lecturing, consulting and teaching the ancient study of handwriting.

I faxed LaVina a selection of Joan's letters, from as early as 1923, thru to 1945. It was a well-rounded view of a young starlet, determined to make it, thru to the pinnacle of her career, a movie star, writing from the set of, *Mildred Pierce* - But, remember...Lavina had absolutely no clue as to who wrote these letters.

The following report is what LaVina saw in Joan's handwriting. Her personality, her emotions, her good points and her not so good points. It is so eerily close to Joan's personality, that any skeptics reading this introduction would surely be swayed with LaVina's findings.

"I could spend hours analyzing this person and still not get the full depth. Emotional responsiveness is very high which means that the person will respond to situations with feelings. It also appears that the depth of emotion and feelings will be deeply absorbed and will not fade easily. It is difficult working from fax copies to be 100% clear on this attribute, but this is what the copies indicate. This person has a strong desire to be expressive.

She feels deeply and has lasting emotional memories. Anger, joy and happiness, all last a long time. Some of the memories and permanent and she never forgets any of the lessons life has taught her. She stores memories as emotions. What she see, tastes, smells, touches or hears, reminds her of similar experiences she as had before. The emotional feeling connected with these memories then determines how she sometimes reacts.

There are some of the preliminary traits that are prevalent throughout the years. The high emotional responsiveness and the depth of feelings with the strong desire to be expressive are found throughout. The spacing between words indicates a need for their own space.

Mental processes are analytical; this person is a very quick learner. Her own ideas are more important to her than the ideas of others. At times even unwilling to consider the merits of views, ideas and practices of others, even to the point at times of being defensive. As with a lot of intelligent people, their interests are varied and vast, sometimes causing conflicts. There is conflict of interests found in all the writing, more so in the later years than the early ones.

Amazing enthusiasm, perseverance, and determination is found throughout the writings from 1923-1945. Fluidity, sense of timing, desire to express is strong and consistent. This person is very goal directed and driven. She directs her mental energies toward the fulfillment of her aspirations. Her outlook is eager and optimistic. Enthusiasm will carry her along. Cheerful anticipation grows the closer she approaches her goals. Feeling halfway about something is impossible for her.

Her enthusiasm will not only make tasks more enjoyable but creates interest in others and assures their support. With her eagerness and zeal she is able to inspire others. She makes them believers in her cause. She has a gregarious flair!

An infectious sense of humor is found. She has the ability to laugh and enjoy the good times. She is able to see the funny side of life. Others often laugh with her because her humor is contagious. With an awareness of how amusing she, herself, can be in her foibles and follies she can chuckle at herself without loss of self-esteem.

However, she will always do it with good taste and cultural tendencies. In her manner, speech and character, she is instinctively refined. She abhors coarseness and vulgarity. Beauty in all its forms moves her emotionally. She has a real feeling for harmony and wants things to feel "right" in every area of her life. She desires elegant living, gracious forms, gently manners and peaceful, pleasant surroundings. She loves gracefulness in all it forms and quality and atmosphere are essential. She possesses a deep appreciation for all that is beautiful in art and nature. Art can take many forms from the canvas to the stage. Her taste is highly developed and she has a great sense of order and proportion. She wants things in the right place in harmony with their environment. She wants to be part of an attractive world and has a sensual nature.

The writer is physically motivated and inclined to express herself in terms of bodily activity. Her initial reaction to anything is usually on the physical level and she performs best when she can act rather than think. She has a lot of nervous energy at times and will have many projects going at one time. She is compelled to try hard in every area of her life. Making a good impression is important to her.

She desires to gain approval from others in both her conduct and her accomplishments. She wants to be thought of well by others and she wants to think well of herself. She will depend upon herself to form her opinions. She thinks and acts according to her own beliefs and is her own authority. She expects others to be as diligent and when they are not, she

184

can become irritated and frustrated. When she does become upset either through frustration or temporary strains those around her will know it.

In the later years of writing, some resentment strokes were found. Frequently she would feel indignant toward others, from a sense of being insulted, offended, or put off in some form or manner. Could have been a feeling of being piqued about the real or imagined encroachment on her time, her possessions or her privacy. Overall, she will rise above these tendencies with her over whelming enthusiasm and gregarious spirit."

The High Price of Fame

"I never go out unless I look like the movie star, Joan Crawford. If you want to see the girl next door, go next door!"

- Joan Crawford.

It's fascinating to think that many people actually had *the* Joan Crawford as their pen pal. A mere fan would have little chance of a relationship like that with their favorite actor of today. Try it and the one piece of correspondence likely to come your way is a restraining order labeling you a "stalker."

It's naive to think that Joan Crawford only ever received positive, fan worship letters from her fans. Her main address, 426 North Bristol Avenue, was her home, and the majority of the mail was sent to her there. The studio safety net of having her letters opened and sorted to weed out the negative correspondence just wasn't an option because she openly encouraged people to write to her at her home address.

Were people really that different back then? Less aggressive, maybe? Less psychotic? No, of course not! There had to have been hate mail sent, and knowing Joan, she probably responded to it, thanking them graciously for their 'constructive criticism.'

The only documented account of any threat toward Joan Crawford wasn't until her career had ended. In 1974, she received a death threat via a phone message. The FBI were called in to monitor her apartment but after months of nothing eventuating, they left their post, advising her to update her security devices. Joan listened, spending some $3,500 on new locks and an advanced alarm system; it gave her piece of mind and added protection. She never received another threat on her life.

Joan Crawford may have been the only star insistent on responding to her own fan mail but she certainly wasn't the only star receiving mailbags full of letters. For the month of April 1928, *The It Girl*, Clara Bow, received almost 34,000 letters. She employed three full time secretaries to respond, at a cost of $450. The cost of stamps, for that one-month, was a whopping, $2,100. Her closest male counterpart was Charles 'Buddy' Rogers, with 19,618 letters. Douglas Fairbanks Sr. came in second, at 8,000 letters. Surprisingly, the original debonair swashbuckler's main rival had four legs and a tail!

Rin Tin Tin, equaled Fairbanks' fan mail in 1928, consistently receiving approx. 8,000 letters per month, for the year. Fairbanks found humor in his main rival, but Donald O'Connor found his competition with a mule degrading to the point that he walked out of a successful film franchise because of it. After making six films with Francis the Talking Mule, O'Connor relinquished the lead role to Mickey Rooney because Francis, (the mule), was receiving more fan mail than he was!

In 1933, Walt Disney released fan mail figures for his beloved, Mickey Mouse. The fictional creature received 800,000 letters for the year, averaging an astounding 66,000 per month! All of them were addressed to Mickey personally. Very few, if any were addressed to Walt Disney himself.

Shirley Temple was the youngest star to receive record numbers of fan mail. By 1936, at the tender age of seven, the little cherub-faced starlet was receiving an average of 60,000 letters per month. During WWII, Betty Grable averaged 30,000 letters per month, most of those letters came from lovesick boys serving in the army. After the war, Roy Rogers took top honors, receiving close to 75,000 letters per month. His horse Trigger wasn't forgotten about either, he received close to two hundred, all personally addressed to him.

Statistics show that close to three-quarters of all fan mail is written by women, but when men do put pen to paper and write to their favorite star, it's to request one of two things. They either want a date, or they completely skip the courting and go straight to the marriage proposal.
An example of a few of the more entertaining, requests that stars have received over the years are as follows:

To early screen star, Kathlyn Williams - Circa 1916: "Dear Miss Williams, You are my favorite moving picture actress. I would appreciate so much if you would give me one of your old automobiles, any one. I wouldn't care how small."

To Una Merkel - Circa 1933: Following a request for a signed photo, this fan wrote another letter stating, "Do not send picture. Am moving and decided I don't want it." Una Merkel responded, "Picture is sent. You'll take it and like it!"

To Glenn Ford - Circa 1946: "I am 22, pretty, but I never saved my money. You did. That is the real reason I would like to marry you. Please let me know soon, as I have also written to Dick Powell and Larry Parks."

It's unfortunate, but completely understandable, that most of today's stars choose to employ fan services to open their mail and respond to it for them. Not because of the sheer volume they receive, but mostly due to the constant threat of psychotic fans who either hate them or even love them, to death! - The first studio fan mail operation was set up by Jack Tamkin, in 1962. His staff responded to between 100,000 and 200,000 fan letters a month. Representing many celebrities, all mail is read and sorted into three categories. Most responses simply require a standard facsimile signature of the star in question. However, other letters from sick or disadvantaged children will be forwarded to the stars agent, for further investigation. Any threatening letters are recorded on a database and sent directly to the LAPD's specialist stalking division.

Ben Stiller recently admitted to paying people to shield him from his fan mail, saying, *"I pay a huge chunk of money to my agent and publicity people to shield me from my fan mail. I don't even want to know how many letters I get. I don't see fan mail as a good thing. It always makes me think of stalkers."*

On the other hand, Viggo Mortensen, who has been so inundated with letters since starring in *The Lord of the Rings* trilogy, recently explained, via his website, how he would be dealing with the influx of new autograph requests:

"Over the years I have made the effort to read and answer every piece of fan mail that I received. Lately, however, the volume of mail has increased significantly making it practically impossible to keep up with it all and respond to each piece personally. Although I am grateful for the favorable response that those of us involved in the 'Lord of the Rings' trilogy have had, it is simply a bit overwhelming. I find that I have little or no time left for other pursuits and have little free time left for art projects or for spending time with friends and family.

Therefore, as I do not wish to have my mail answered for me by others, I have no choice but to say that I will no longer be accepting fan mail after October 31, 2002. Please do not send anymore letters or cards as it will not be answered. I will, however, continue to honor requests for autographs in person, as I have always done. I thank you for your support and kind thoughts."

That statement really confirms the time and commitment that Joan Crawford put in to answering all of her correspondence. When managing a busy life and career, it's virtually impossible to commit to such an overwhelming task, but she most certainly did, she would never consider disappointing her fans by ignoring them.

One modern day exception to the rule is Tom Cruise. At a recent London premiere of his film, *The Last Samurai*, he satisfied the autograph and photo requests of his devoted fans holding up his own premiere by an hour. *People Online* reported that Cruise spent over two hours, walking around Leicester Square, signing close to 1,000 autographs, posing for even more photographs, and happily chatting to disbelieving friends and relatives on cell phones that were offered him.

Prior to his Premiere, Cruise said, *"If anyone shows up and wants my autograph, they can have it."* More than 5,000 people turned out to see the superstar in the midst of a London winter and he stuck to his word. After the marathon session, Cruise joked, *"I will probably start before dawn (next time) and work my way through. We'll have a marathon!"*

Still, the scary stories of obsessive fans have stars such as Elizabeth Taylor, John Travolta, Robert Redford and Cher turning to Gavin de Becker, a studio security specialist to oversee any potentially dangerous admirers. He keeps FBI-like files and classifies fans according to the risk they pose to the star in question.

History has proven that no amount of security will stop an obsessed fan from getting to their idol, their victim. One of the most infamous cases of assassination at the hands of a fan, was of course the tragic death of John Lennon. After leaving the Dakota apartment building earlier one afternoon to go to a recording session at the Record Plant, Mark David Chapman, approached Lennon and asked him to autograph his album. Lennon autographed the album and went to the studio. It's safe to say, that very autograph that Lennon gave to Chapman, was his last.

Chapman lay in wait for several hours until Lennon returned to the luxurious Dakota apartment building in New York City. He waited for Lennon's wife, Yoko Ono, to pass first, even saying hello to her as she entered the building. As Lennon passed, Chapman emerged from the darkness and shot him four times in the back. Lennon was rushed to hospital in the back of a police car but later died.

Chapman expressed hearing voices in his head telling him to kill the former, Beatle. He succeeded. He's now serving a 20-year to life sentence in Attica prison. Chapman was eligible for parole in October 2000, but a heartfelt letter written by Lennon's widow, Yoko Ono, and presented to the parole board, helped in that request being denied. A second parole hearing in October 2002, was also denied. Chapman was eligible for another parole hearing, his third, in October 2004, again he was denied.

It was a traumatic end to the year, when on December 30, 1999, John Lennon's former Beatle band mate, the late, George Harrison and his wife, Olivia were the victims of multiple stab wounds in their own home. An intruder broke into their heavily secure, Oxfordshire mansion, stabbing Harrison in the chest, penetrating and deflating his lung. Harrison's wife, Olivia, received superficial wounds as she helped fight off the attacker, finally hitting him over the head with a lamp, disabling him until police arrived.

Michael Abram, 34, was diagnosed with severe paranoid schizophrenia and found to be not guilty on both counts of attempted murder. He believed all four members of *The Beatles* to be practitioners of black magic with George Harrison being the leader 'who got inside his head and tormented him.' Abram's was admitted to a mental hospital, indefinitely.

The brutal 1989 death of 21-year-old actress Rebecca Schaeffer is a classic example of a fan so obsessed with a star, they'll stop at nothing, even murder. Robert Bardo, also 21, was an unemployed fast food worker, who flooded Rebecca with love letters from the moment she appeared as the fresh-faced sister of Pam Dawber on the hit TV show, *My Sister Sam.* He covered his walls with photos of the young actress and even mailed a letter to his sister in Tennessee, telling her "if I can't have her, no one else will." Just days after mailing that chilling letter, Bardo boarded a bus from Tucson to Hollywood, determined to find, and kill, Rebecca Schaeffer.

Immediately after arriving in California, he went to the obvious first choice, her agent. After calling her agent's office he was angered further when they refused to release her address to him. With her picture in hand, he roamed the local streets, asking innocent passersby if they knew where she lived. In the end, he went to a professional. For $250 he hired a private detective to find her address for him. With the information he so desperately wanted, Bardo, went straight to 120 N. Sweetzer Ave, rang her doorbell, and without hesitation, shot her at close range as she opened the door.

As neighbors heard Rebecca's screams, they clamored to help try to stop the bleeding, as her body lay wedged between the door and its frame. Other witnesses saw Bardo jog down a nearby alley and seemingly disappear. Rebecca was rushed to Cedars Sinai Medical Center, and despite frantic medical treatment, her injuries were massive. She died some 30 minutes later.

What's amazing that during the time that Rebecca Schaeffer was shot and killed, Bardo had calmly boarded a bus back to Tucson. It was a call to 911 by several concerned motorists to report a guy running amongst traffic on Interstate 10 that led to his arrest. Convicted of capital murder in a non-jury courtroom, it was December 20, 1991, that Bardo was sentenced to life in prison, without parole.

His cold statement to Judge Dino Fulgoni on the day of his sentencing shows no hint of remorse, *"The idea I killed her for fame is totally ridiculous. I do realize the magnitude of what I've done. I don't think it needs to be compounded by a bunch of lies because she's an actress."*

Madonna has had her fair share of crazed fans, luckily none proved harmful but the intent was most certainly there. Even with the extensive security measures that stars take to guard their homes, there are times when that security is questioned when an intruder can scale the outer walls of the mansion and get within dangerous reach. Robert Hoskins, did just that, scaling the walls of Madonna's Hollywood Hills mansion and leaving threatening notes on her front door. One note, threatened to slash her throat if she didn't marry him. His third attempt at scaling the wall was his last, he was shot by a bodyguard and sentenced to 10 and a half years with psychiatric services.

Michael J. Fox received thousands of fan letters a week, none of them more scary than the 6,000 letters he received from Tina Ledbetter. Her demands were that he leave his wife for her, if he, didn't she vowed his career would fade away. A threat that could mean any number of things.

When her letters went unanswered, she sent him a box of rabbit droppings. That was the final straw, Fox called the police and Ledbetter was taken to a psychiatric facility. To this day she vows to get her revenge.

Talk show host, David Letterman was the target of Margaret M. Ray, a woman who successfully broke into his Connecticut home while he was away. She slept in his bed, watched television, she even drove his Porsche. Her failure to pay a toll whilst driving the luxury car and claiming to be his wife when questioned, led to her arrest.

She was sentenced to 10 months in prison with a further 14 months in a state mental hospital. Her treatment failed her, just months after completing these sentences; she was back in court, charged with stalking astronaut, Story Musgrave. She ended her own torment on October 5, 1998, by walking to the edge of the railroad tracks near her home, where she knelt down in the path of an oncoming train. She was killed instantly.

Singer, Anne Murray, was the target of a phone stalker, a farmer, named Robert Kieling. He repeatedly called the country star, up to 263 times, in a six-month period. His reason? He wanted to marry her. He was arrested and charged with harassment.

Some stars are so terrified after being the victim of a stalker, they've taken up arms themselves. Clint Eastwood, Jerry Lewis and the late, Michael Landon all carried guns after experiencing an episode with a crazed fan. One fan, got within reach of Landon and whispered, *"You'll have to look over your shoulder the rest of your life."*

It's not always the stars themselves who are threatened; even spouses and especially children are the prey of would be kidnappers and killers. It was a threat to Jerry Lewis' daughter that finally saw him call the police and see that Gary Benson was arrested and charged under the stalking law.

Ironically, it was an inside connection, a favor for an employee, that caused the terror to unfold in the Lewis household. A housekeeper asked Lewis to 'pull a few strings' and do a background check on her new fiancée, he managed to get hold of a protracted police file and gave it to her, just as she asked. She told Benson what Lewis had done, enraged, he started a string of phone calls, at first threatening Lewis' life, and finally the life of his six year old daughter.

The housekeeper was fired and even despite the psychotic threats to Lewis and his family, she still went through with the marriage to Benson. They have since divorced.

It was three long years of constant threats that had the legendary comedian spend up to $80,000 a month for added security protection. He was eventually diagnosed as a chronic schizophrenic and sentenced to six years in prison, not surprisingly; most of that sentence was spent in mental wards. At a parole hearing in 1998, Lewis testified, *"I want the system to work for me and others, I want to keep him in jail."*

Benson was denied parole and continued to have homicidal episodes directed toward the comedian. He confessed to a psychiatrist that he hears voices telling him to kill Lewis. *"Yes, I am convinced that he will kill me if he ever gets out,"* Lewis said.

John Hinckley Jr. put a bizarre twist on what a fan will do to get the attention of a star. His 1981 attempted assassination of President Ronald Reagan, was carried out to impress his favorite actress, Jodie Foster. - His incarceration in a mental facility is eerily made easier by the photos of her that cover the walls of his room.

A seven woman, five man jury, sentenced Jonathan Norman to 25 years to life on June 16, 1998 for a crime that he luckily, was prevented from carrying out. His sick sexual obsession for movie director Steven Spielberg was recounted in detail, as a visibly shaken, sometimes tearful Spielberg told the court of his fear of this supposed 'admirer.'

"No one before has come into my life in a way to do me harm or my family harm" he sobbed. *"I really felt - and I still to this day feel - I am prey to this individual.'* He went on to tell the crowded courtroom how he felt when he learned of Norman's plan to rape him, *'I was at first stunned and then terrified. I reacted to the information, at first, with disbelief, and then I became quite frightened."*

When arrested, Norman was caught with a box containing handcuffs, duct tape and a diary containing details of Spielberg's family and associates. *"I was concerned that he brought so many handcuffs',* Spielberg stated to the court, *'I could only speculate that what he wanted to do to me, he might also want to do to someone else in the family. The razor knife could have been used for.... you know."* Spielberg slowly ran his finger across his throat to demonstrate.

Princess Caroline of Monaco, the daughter of the late, Grace Kelly, was herself targeted by a stalker in 1993. He wrote her constant letters, telling her how much he wanted to photograph her in Cleopatra like poses. When his letters went unanswered, he became more persistent, more threatening. His final letters stating that he would kill himself in front of the Princess and her young children if she went through with her plans to wed, Vincent London. She married, and thankfully so far, there has been no such attempt.

Veteran CBS news anchor, Dan Rather, was attacked in January of 1997, whilst innocently strolling down New York's luxurious Park Avenue. William Tager, had been stalking the newsman, followed him, punching him in the face from behind. A stunned Rather, ran to the safety of a nearby building, Tager chased him and was subsequently arrested. Tager confessed in a psychiatric evaluation that he attacked Rather and even considered crippling him, changing his mind at the last minute. In a move that can now only be viewed as a horrible mistake, he was not considered a continual threat and was released back into society. He is now serving a 25-year prison term for stalking and killing a stagehand.

This deadly obsession that some fans have with celebrities, doesn't end with movie or television stars. Sports personalities have the same public exposure because of television coverage. Tennis ace, Monica Seles, was attacked, in Hamburg, Germany, whilst playing a game with her main rival, Steffi Graf.

The match was at a stage where Seles was winning. If she won the match, she would dethrone Graf as the number one women's tennis player, taking her place at the top. In a similar parallel to the Jodie Foster/Ronald Reagan case, Gunther Parch hurled himself onto the court as Seles toweled down between sets, stabbing her in the back with a kitchen knife.

As Seles' white tennis shirt soaked up her blood, Parch was taken away. His 1993 sentencing of two years was ludicrous with the judge stating that she believed that his intention was to 'only' harm Seles, not kill her. After a long break of almost two years, Seles once again resumed playing on the women's tennis circuit. Sadly, she has never again been as close to being number one as she was on the day of her attack.

More recently, Oscar winner, Gwyneth Paltrow broke down when giving evidence in court against her stalker, Dante Soiu. Beginning in March 1999, Paltrow began receiving e-mails, letters and packages of a sexually explicit nature. When the correspondence went unanswered, Soiu showed up twice outside her parents Los Angeles home looking for her. After FBI agents went to his Ohio home to warn him to stop, he persisted even more, sending her flowers, candy, pizza and pornography along with sexually explicit letters.

Paltrow testified that Soiu's obsession with her, *"gave her nightmares."* The judge, Robert O'Neill, found Dante Soiu to be legally insane and sentenced him to an appropriate psychiatric facility for rehabilitation.

Thankfully, former President, Bill Clinton, signed a revised legislation in 1996 that strengthened and enforced the seriousness of what it is to be a stalker. It is now a federal crime to cross state lines with the intent of harassing another person. If that person, the victim, is injured as a result of a stalker, the punishment can range anywhere between five to twenty years in jail. If that person, the victim, dies as a result of a stalker, justice is now rightfully done with a lifetime conviction.

Cast-aphrocies!

*"Joan Crawford behaved like a star. Some do, some don't...You know, when Joan came on the set, **somebody** came on the set."*
- Rosalind Russell.

As with many actors, there are occasions when a role has been lost, for one reason or another. Whether it be a conflict in personalities, contract negotiations, illness, pregnancy, any number of factors, a lost role can be a make or break career moment for the actor who turns it down, as well as the actor who takes it on.

There are many instances of major film roles being overlooked by an actor who's had the golden opportunity of saying yes to it, only to turn it down to the good fortune of someone else.

It's a judgment call, not every script reads as well as it can eventually be on film and it takes more than an actor to see that potential. More often than not, those classic roles that legendary actors such as, Judy Garland, Vivien Leigh, Humphrey Bogart and Ingrid Bergman made famous, were all roles that were offered to another actor before them. Hard to imagine, isn't it?

Considering many of the actors who went on to make the roles famous were not first choices, it makes one consider how in tune studio casting directors were at their jobs. Make sure you're sitting down for some of these prime examples; fate stepped in and thankfully diverted some definite cast-astrophies!

Shirley Temple was originally set to play Dorothy, in, *The Wizard of Oz*, however 20th Century Fox refused to lend her to MGM so the part was passed along to one of their own contract players, Judy Garland. In other *Wizard of Oz* casting choices, Buddy Ebsen actually filmed scenes as 'The Tin Man," but was forced to pull out due to a severe reaction to the silver paint used on his skin. Jack Haley refilmed his scenes and went on to become best known for his portrayal as the lovable "Tin Man" who longed to have a heart. In the one "Oz" casting decision that actually could have worked, W.C Fields was initially offered the role as "The Wizard," however he wanted a higher salary and MGM weren't willing to accommodate his demands. Frank Morgan took the role, and again, is best remembered for his role as the lovable, but cranky, "Wizard of Oz."

In another classic 1939 production, hundreds of young actresses auditioned for the role of Scarlett O'Hara in *Gone With The Wind*. In one of the longest screen tests in the history of motion pictures, David O Selznick, shot close to thirty hours of test footage at a cost of $105,000. The price of the screen test footage alone was the average budget of an entire B grade picture. Such well-known faces as, Bette Davis, Paulette Goddard, Katharine Hepburn, Susan Hayward, and yes, even Joan did a screen test for Scarlett. Norma Shearer was originally cast as Scarlett, however she withdrew from the part in July of 1938. Her reason? - She received so much negative fan mail from fans of the Margaret Mitchell best seller; she just couldn't go through with the part. I don't know about you, but I can't imagine anyone but Vivien Leigh saying that immortal line, "Oh, fiddle dee dee."

Cyd Charise was handed the coveted role in *An American In Paris*, however, having just found out she was pregnant, she burst into tears when she realized she'd have to decline the part. Leslie Caron stepped into her shoes, literally, and danced her own way into Hollywood musical history.

At one point, Warner Brothers actually considered recasting the three lead roles in *Casablanca*. Picture this! Dennis Morgan was to replace Humphrey Bogart, Ann Sheridan was to replace Ingrid Bergman and Ronald Reagan was to replace Paul Henreid. As if that wasn't enough, George Raft was offered the part of Rick in *Casablanca* and Sam Spade in *The Maltese Falcon,* only to pass on both! Ironically, Humphrey Bogart is best remembered as 'Sam' and 'Rick' in both of these films.

Cary Grant turned down the role of Professor Henry Higgins in the film version of *My Fair Lady*. It was a role that Rex Harrison eventually took, and did well enough to be awarded an Oscar for his efforts.

Billy Wilder's first choice to play forgotten movie queen, Norma Desmond, in *Sunset Boulevard*, was Mae West. She not only rejected the role, she was highly insulted that she was even thought of to play a has-been, even if it was on screen. Mary Pickford and Pola Negri were also offered the role, long before Gloria Swanson was even a consideration. It was George Cukor who suggested her for the part. Again, Swanson is best remembered for her role as the insane actress who takes a somewhat twisted liking to a handsome screenwriter, played by, William Holden.

One of Joan's bigger judgment mistakes was to turn down the part of Karen Holmes in *From Here to Eternity* (1953) - Her reason? - She hated the costumes! - Of course, Deborah Kerr took the role and went on to create one of the sexiest love scenes in movie history with co-star Burt Lancaster. It's hard to imagine why Joan would pass up the opportunity to roll around on a beach with Burt Lancaster, but her repulsion of the planned costumes was enough for her to overlook that perk. She sent the script back to Columbia as a Joan Crawford reject.

The following list of both film and television roles are listed in alphabetical order, by title. The reasons why Joan and any given project didn't make it are noted underneath the title.

A Certain Young Man (1928) -
Marceline Day was given the role of 'Phyllis' in this Ramon Novarro film after Joan was considered 'unsuitable'.

Airport '77 (1977) -
Olivia De Havilland took the role of 'Emily Livingston' after Joan passed on the role because there was insufficient rehearsal time.

Batman (TV - 1966) -
Several rumors circulated about Joan appearing as a guest villainous in this popular television series, however, for unknown reasons, it was never finalized.

Biography of a Bachelor Guy (1935) -
No solid reason given for Joan not getting the role of 'Marion Forsythe," only that she was 'unsuitable.'

Butterflies are Free (1972) -
Joan turned down the role of "Mrs. Baker."

Caged (1950) -
Agnes Moorehead and Eleanor Parker took the roles that were initially pitched to Joan and Bette Davis.

Cannon (TV - 1975) -
Joan Fontaine took the role of "Thelma Cain," after Joan turned it down, due to time constraints.

The Christian (1934) -
Screen writer, P. J. Wolfson was given an assignment to write a story for Joan and Clark Gable. For reasons unknown, the project was shelved.

Conflict (1945) -

Joan refused this Warner Brothers film because of script conflict. Her character was written to lose her lover, played by Humphrey Bogart, to her younger sister, played by Alexis Smith. The final straw for Joan was reading that her character would be murdered by the end of the film. She declined the role.

Cry Havoc (1943) -

Joan went on suspension for not taking the role touted for her in *Cry Havoc,* she was prepared to take the studio penalty, rather than attach her name to a bad picture.

Dinner at Eight (1933) -

Madge Evans ended up playing the role of 'The Girl."

Elegance (1934) -

This MGM project was shelved after Joan and her co-star Clifton Webb clashed too often during rehearsals.

Ethan Frome (1947) -

Another project written for Joan and Bette Davis. It also appears to have been shelved.

Every Day is Mother's Day (TV - 1966) -

Joan signed a contract for $7,500 for a ten-day shoot with Hope Pictures, however the project was shelved and never made.

Ex -Wife (1930) -

MGM bought the rights to Ursula Parrott's story about a divorced woman who lives a life of sexual freedom. The studio had Joan in mind to play the lead, however when Norma Shearer saw the script, she demanded to be given the part. This move certainly helped to build the long-standing rivalry that existed between the two actresses, especially after Norma Shearer went on to win the Oscar for her performance. *Ex-Wife,* was released as, *The Divorcee.*

Follies (1972) -

Peter Bogdanovich was brought in to direct this film, based around the demolition of an old movie studio. Joan, Bette Davis, Elizabeth Taylor, Richard Burton, Debbie Reynolds, Gloria Swanson, Janet Leigh, Anne Jeffreys, Shelley Winters and Frederic March had all signed to appear, however the money people backed out and the project was canceled.

From Here to Eternity (1953) -
As mentioned previously, Joan passed on the role of Karen Holmes, because of her dislike for the planned wardrobe. They weren't willing to change the designs to accommodate Joan so the role went to Deborah Kerr.

The Fugitive Kind (Stage -1940) -
This Tennessee Williams play was offered to Joan but she turned it down, calling the part of 'Myra Torrence', "low and common." Tallulah Bankhead turned it down after Joan. Miriam Hopkins eventually took the part.

Gone with the Wind (1939) -
As previously mentioned, Joan auditioned, (along with almost every other actress in Hollywood), for the role of Scarlett O'Hara.

Great Day (1930) -
After a few weeks of filming and $280,000 invested, *Great Day* was shut down upon the direct orders of Louis B. Mayer. Joan was to play a baby vamp from the south and after seeing the dailies, she was horrified at her performance, *"I can't play an ingénue,"* she told Mayer. He agreed and abandoned the rest of filming. It was a costly mistake but the decision to abandon a film in the midst of production is not made lightly, the initial loss, was thought to be a wiser decision than continuing the filming.

The Hard Way (1942) -
MGM wanted to make this film with Joan, Clark Gable and Lana Turner, however Warner Brothers weren't agreeable to their offer of $100,000 to buy the rights. Warner's made the film the following year with Dennis Morgan, Ida Lupino and Joan Leslie.

The Heavenly Body (1943) -
Hedy Lamarr took this role after Joan didn't like the part.

Her Cardboard Lover (1942) -
In another time of suspension for Joan, she was punished by MGM for turning down the role in this film. Norma Shearer took the part instead.

Hollywood Revue of 1933 (aka Hollywood Party of 1934) -
Joan performed *Black Diamond* and portrayed a harlot who sleeps her way to the top in various sleazy Paris nightclubs. Her performance was left on the cutting room floor. Stan Laurel, Oliver Hardy, Jimmy Durante and

Luper Velez were some of the major Hollywood stars that made the final cut.

A House is Not a Home (1964) -
Joan went after the role of "Polly Adler" with fierce determination, however, Shelley Winters was given the part.

Hush...Hush, Sweet Charlotte (1964) -
See the related "letters section" relating to the casting drama surrounding this film.

Infidelity (1938) -
This was to be Joan's first film with MGM after signing her new contract. With the plot surrounding an adulteress husband, Joan was to play the long-suffering, cheated wife. The subject of infidelity was considered to be offensive to audiences of the time so the script was reworked. Even with the considerable changes, the project was shelved for good.

The Joan Crawford Theater (TV - 1959) -
Some publicity was leaked about Joan doing a half hour television series, however the idea fizzled out and never eventuated.

Kind Sir (Stage -1952) -
After begging to audition for the role in this play, Joan got an audition and was so good; she was offered the role on the spot. Despite her achievement, she politely declined the part. She simply wanted to test herself to see if she could pull off a live reading with enough conviction to at least be offered the role. She did, and she went home happy. Mary Martin ended up taking the role.

Lisbon (1953) -
Paramount bought this script specifically for Joan, but the story outline of losing her leading man to a younger girl, didn't sit well with her ego. When Director, Irving Rapper, declined a script revision and Joan refused to compromise so the project was shelved.

The Merry Widow (1935) -
Joan was to star in this remake, only if it were to be a drama. MGM were in two minds about whether to turn it into a musical or a drama. It was remade in 1935 with Jeanette McDonald in Joan's coulda been role, needless to say, it was a musical.

Madame Curie (1943) -
Joan put in a request to star in this film but the studio had Greer Garson in mind for the role.

Never Goodbye (1943) -
Joan turned this Warner Brothers script down shortly before taking her Oscar winning role in *Mildred Pierce*.

Night Shift (1943) -
Another Warner Brothers script turned down by Joan.

Outcast Lady (1934) -
Joan was briefly considered for this role before it went to Constance Bennett.

The Paradine Case (1947) -
Both Joan and Vivien Leigh were offered the role of "Mrs. Parradine", in this Alfred Hitchcock production. However, first choice, Alida Valli, was eventually issued her Italian work permit and the studios back up plan to use either Joan or Vivien Leigh was abandoned.

Parnell (1937) -
Joan refused to star alongside Clark Gable in this one, so Myrna Loy was her second choice replacement.

Peyton Place (TV - 1968) -
Joan volunteered to step in to Dorothy Malone's reoccurring role when she became ill. The show's producers thanked her for her offer and used Lola Albright instead.

Portrait in Black (1960) -
Joan bought the rights to this film in 1959, with the intention of playing the lead role herself. After shopping around with that very proposal, she was unable to get the funding to get the project into production. Frustrated, she sold the rights and the role of "Sheila Cabot" was eventually played by Lana Turner.

The Prize Fighter and the Lady (1933) -
This was another project pitched to Joan and Clark Gable.

Random Harvest (1942) -
Joan asked to be cast as the lead in this film but she was passed over by MGM for their first choice, Greer Garson.

Reckless (1935) -
Jean Harlow replaced Joan in this musical with co-star, William Powell.

Red-Headed Woman (1932) -
Jean Harlow also replaced Joan in this production.

Return to Peyton Place (1961) -
Eleanor Parker and Mary Astor ended up taking the two mother roles that were originally written (once again) for Joan and Bette Davis.

Sex and Mrs. Macado (1963) -
Joan casually mentioned this film as an upcoming project on an interview with Merv Griffin, however, it never materialized.

The Shopworn Angel (1938) -
Margaret Sullivan took the role that Joan turned down, he co-star was James Stewart.

The Single Standard (1929) -
For reasons unknown, Greta Garbo replaced Joan in this production.

Sleuth (Stage - 1972) -
Joan was offered the lead role but due to her advanced age and fear of live performances, she declined the offer.

Sons of Satan aka I Bastardi (1968) --
A contractual disagreement meant shelving two would be Italian films, *Sons of Satan aka I Bastardi* and *You'll Hang My Love*, both starring Joan.

The Spiral Staircase (TV - 1961) -
Once again, Joan bought the rights here, selling them at a later date. She was not involved in any future production of the film.

Superman - The Movie (1978) -
It was shortly after Joan's death that the producers of *Superman: The Movie* put in a call to her agent, offering her the part of Ma Kent. It would have been her biggest role in years. However, the call came too late. After being informed of her death, Phyllis Thaxter was cast as Superman's mother.

The Talker (1925) -
Joan was going to be loaned to First National Pictures for a small role as "The secretary" or "Ruth" in this production. For reasons unknown, she played neither character.

There Goes Romance (1934) -
MGM purchased this for Joan but it was never made.

Three Comrades (1938) -
Joseph Mankiewicz offered this role to Joan but she turned it down with her excuse being that the male leads dominated the film. Margaret Sullavan didn't agree with her, she took the role, and was nominated for an Academy Award for her efforts.

Three Hearts for Julia (1943) -
Joan refused this role on the basis that her proposed co-star, Melvyn Douglas wasn't a strong enough box office star for the male lead. Anne Southern took Joan's role.

Time to Sing (Unknown year) -
Another Joan and Bette Davis film that never eventuated.

Unashamed (1932) -
Helen Twelvetrees was cast in the role of "Joan Ogden" opposite co-star, Robert Young. MGM initially thought of Joan for the role.

Women Behind Bars (Unknown year) -
Another Joan and Bette Davis film, this time a prison drama. It never happened.

Remembering Joan

"I love playing bitches. There's a lot of bitch in every woman...a lot in every man."

- Joan Crawford.

It is somewhat sad to think that we have entered a time where many of the treasured friends and peers of Joan Crawford have since passed on. In doing the research for this book, I tracked down the few remaining people who did have an association with her, one way or another, and I asked them how they remembered Joan Crawford, today.

Several of the people interviewed for this section never met Joan, however, they are experts in the field of Hollywood history, and they have their own opinions on why Joan Crawford remains, the ultimate star...

On January 4, 2003, I received a letter from a woman who did know Joan, Betsy Palmer. She played 'Carol Lee Phillips' in, *Queen Bee,* and her memories of her friend and coworker were still as strong and as loving as ever.

Dear Michelle ~

Thank you for your sweet note regarding Joan - She and I remained friends till the end (if indeed there is an end) of her life. Great lady, and we had a lovely mutual respect of one another.

Unfortunately, I never saved any of her Christmas greetings or other notes - I'm not a collector of anything, not even my own memorabilia - Sorry! My memories are in my head: Thank you for writing a loving project about her. You probably saw the documentary about Ms Crawford by Peter Fitzgerald. I was in it and spoke lovingly of her.

- Always, Betsy Palmer.

This book and its purpose is to show what an unusually close relationship Joan Crawford shared with her fans. In the year 2000, an 88-

year-old woman, known only as 'Elizabeth,' told of her own cherished memories of a very young starlet who became a movie star, Joan Crawford:

Joan was in her first years in Hollywood. My father and I ran a snack bar concession down below the country club on Santa Monica beach. Even then, she was making a name for herself in pictures and we knew exactly whom we were serving. She wore 'short' stylish beach dresses over her suit, and she was covered head to foot with millions of freckles!

She was always friendly and chatty with us; never stuck up. She ordered the same snack every time: A hot dog with nothing on it except loads of mustard, more mustard than it seemed possible to eat and still taste the rest of the sandwich! - It made my mouth pucker even though I was just a little girl and loved mustard, too. Later on, I came to love Joan for her style, relentless courage and her captivating portrayals of strong and fascinating characters on the screen.

But, I will never forget the warm, friendly girl with the beautiful laugh, who didn't wear make up, running to us, all covered with water and freckles and sand, just dying for a hot dog, and making me and my Dad feel like we were the best cooks in California!

Rex Reed related a story that actress, 'Glenda Jackson' had apparently told him, about how Joan had a big dinner party and brought out a huge 20 lb box of chocolates for the guests and found one chocolate missing. She flew into a rage, ordered Christopher dragged out of bed, marched him down the stairs and made him eat the entire box of chocolates until he vomited!

After reading this story and after picturing a warped scene with Joan Crawford and her party guests standing around watching this kid eat the chocolates until he was sick, I decided to write a letter to 'Glenda Jackson' who is now a Member of Parliament in the U.K.

"If this did happen," I wrote, "Why didn't anyone step in and stop it?"

On January 6th, 2003, I received this reply -

Thank you for your letter,

Regretfully, I never had the privilege of meeting Joan Crawford, so the Rex Reed story is sheer fabrication She would have hated this! She wrote to me twice, on both occasions congratulating me on being "awarded the Oscar for best performance by an actress, by the Academy of Motion Pictures" - end quote. Sadly, that was it. She was great and I wish you luck with the book.

- Sincerely, Glenda Jackson.

This is a perfect example to remember whenever you start to believe every little thing that you read in the newspaper or weekly magazines. Not only does Rex Reed's comments tarnish Joan Crawford's name further, but it goes as far as to question the integrity of Glenda Jackson too. Thankfully, Ms. Jackson was kind enough to respond and set the record straight with a dose of something many writers fail to want to know or write about - the truth!

Even the music world has honored Joan's memory, or maybe 'honored' is the wrong word in this case. Whilst Bette Davis is lovingly remembered with the Kim Carnes classic, *Bette Davis Eyes*, Joan's contribution to the music world that spawned a hit for the somewhat off the wall band, 'Blue Oyster Cult', was simply titled, *Joan Crawford.*

With lyrics, repeating, *"Joan Crawford has risen from the grave, Joan Crawford has risen from the grave" and "Christina...Mother's home!"* it's a tongue in cheek "tribute," and I use the word "tribute" loosely, because the song is inspired by Christina's book, *Mommie Dearest.*

In another letter, postmarked May 3, 2003, and sent to me from comedian, Phyllis Diller: she writes:

"I had a couple of sweet letters from Joan Crawford, but I can't find them (15 secretaries later). I only met her once, she was charming - Love, Phyllis Diller.

In an interview with Rusty White, for EInsiders.com, child actor, Gary Gray, remembers a nurturing side to Joan -

"On one of my first movies I was a kid playing hopscotch in the park. I fell down and cut my knee. Before my own mother could get to me, Miss Crawford ran, picked me up, took me into her trailer, cleaned my cut and gave me some chocolate. She did all this without publicizing it or telling anyone. I don't care what anyone says, she had to have had a decent side to her to do what she did for me for no reason other than to help a child who was hurt. Besides, she was dead when that book was written. She wasn't around to defend herself."

Just a few months after Joan's death, Dorothy Manners remembered her friend, Joan Crawford. Her fond remembrance originally appeared in the August 1977 issue of, *Modern Screen* magazine.

*"I think she was the healthiest female I have ever known. Never had colds or even headaches. Which makes her tragic death by heart failure even more shocking to her intimates...
She loved white, hated blue -- 'They named 'the blues' after it.' she said.*

The last time I saw her she cooked me a Mexican "brunch" at her apartment in New York. It was raining buckets outside -- a day for talking and musings. She said, 'I feel sorry for today's stars. They've never learned to enjoy their fame. To them, it is dross. To me it was solid gold all the way.' She was a Great Star. A Great Woman."

Adele Whitely Fletcher's memories of Joan, also appeared in the August 1977 issue of *Modern Screen* magazine -

"Joan worked as hard at being a star, in the studios and in her private life, as she'd worked from the time she was 9 years old -- helping her mother in a laundry, as a waitress, as a salesgirl and as a drudge in the private school where, for her tuition and a pittance, she did all the housework for 30 boarders.

She never let down her star image, even after she left Hollywood for New York. On a busy day she might change costume, hairdo and make-up four times. She went about in a limousine, with a telephone, a crystal vase of fresh flowers and a courteous, liveried chauffeur. At the famous # 21 Club, on her favorite table at the head of the stairway, a bottle of Pepsi Cola always stood prominently beside the flowers. And when word got around she was there, as it always did, she would leave a little early, so she would have time to shake hands, sign autographs and talk with those who waited to see her. Not that there ever was anything "la-de-da" about her. I've seen her scrub floors.

Joan was so vital it's difficult to realize she is no more; vital in voice, thinking and movement. It was with this vitality, among other things, that the chorus girl, Lucille LeSueur, painstakingly shaped herself into Joan Crawford, and Joan Crawford painstakingly shaped herself into the great star she remained until she died -- and the legend she is sure to be. She would have taken the greatest satisfaction from the importance of her death received on radio, television, and in the world press; proof-positive she had remained a great star."

Jonathon Denson, operator of the popular online Joan Crawford website, "Club Crawford," shares his opinion on why Joan Crawford became a star, and why she remains a star, long after her death.

It has been over 25 years since her death, but to this day there are very few stars as famous as Joan Crawford. Her fame is only rivaled by a select few - perhaps Madonna, Cher, and some of her contemporaries. When we think of how long she has been gone compared to her contemporaries (Shearer, Garbo, Davis), it is even more remarkable that her fame is still the greatest. There is possibly no face in the world more instantly recognizable than that of Joan Crawford. What was the one message that Crawford left to the world, through her unforgettable performances, captured forever in the magic of film? It's a spiritual message, one of the most important that life can ever teach us.

People often waste their lives away on their careers and an endless quest to make more money. In the process, they neglect the people they love, and perhaps never find happiness. However, Joan Crawford taught me that when you're unloved, there's nothing to lose. If Crawford was unhappy, I don't believe it was a result of her intense ambitions. She was alone from the very beginning. Her fans were the only love she ever knew. To devote so much of her time to her fans and career was not her downfall. The real tragedy was no one else was ever there for her.

What was Joan Crawford's downfall? If it was not ambition, as implied by many before, then maybe it was her decision to be a mother. Sadly, Crawford became increasingly reliant on alcohol in her later years. She was shy, vulnerable, and insecure. All of this probably stemmed from a family that didn't love her, husbands that didn't love her, and eventually children that didn't love her.

Why Crawford became an alcoholic is easy to understand - it was Hollywood and she was a shy superstar. Drinking helped overcome her fears and some of her unhappiness. I believe her decision to adopt children was sincere - she wanted to be a mother. How much her alcoholism may have affected what kind of mother she was we may never know. Mommie Dearest, the book, represents a great mystery. Christina Crawford's motives for writing the book are questionable - there was obviously a great deal of money to be made by writing the outrageous tell-all biography, which gave the impression to most readers that Joan Crawford bordered on insane.

How much of the book is true is still unknown, although it was likely exaggerated and the abuse was firmly denied by other adopted daughters, Cindy and Cathy. All these years later, the Mommie Dearest scandal has only increased Crawford's fame and popularity - generating interest among many younger generations who otherwise may have never discovered the unique beauty. Stars as great as Joan Crawford never really die.

Beyond the mystery, Joan Crawford has left us some of the greatest screen performances the world has ever known. Many are quick to argue, "Joan was a star, not an actress" (a myth perpetuated by rival Bette Davis), but the truth is Crawford was both. In many ways, her beauty worked against her credibility - she had so much star quality that her acting was often overlooked. She often took star roles instead of acting roles, because she was genuinely afraid of disapproval. However, when Crawford had the courage to defy the star image and attempt a challenging part in a memorable film (such as Humoresque, Strange Cargo, or Rain), put simply, she was timeless.

Another expert opinion comes from Philadelphia filmmaker and digital editor, Mark Toscani. He was first inspired by Joan Crawford when, at the tender age of eight, he saw Whatever Happened to Baby Jane? on TV. According to him, he wondered, "Who is that neat, sharped-boned lady in the wheelchair?" From then on, he has had a canvas on which to paint, and he's been a Joan Crawford connoisseur ever since. These are his thoughts...

Joan Crawford's long film career is staggering. When one considers that most stars last a decade, she lasted five! Here was a unique personality who constantly aimed for perfection. Yet she never portrayed an historical figure, a nun, or a saint. She never played a queen or a conqueror. Her characters were more concerned with paying the gas bill, than with the battlefield. Essentially, she played herself, a poor person from the wrong side of the tracks trying to find happiness in life. Who can't relate to that?

Crawford experienced the typical difficult childhood that most old movie stars seemed to have: poor, no father around, abusive mother, shuffled from school to school. As a child, she developed a love of dancing. Eventually, she made her way to a dance group in New York and was discovered by an MGM talent scout in 1925. In the late twenties, the jazz craze was in full swing. Crawford got her first taste of stardom as a jazz baby in the silent Our Dancing Daughters (1928). Her raw energy and talent shone on the screen. For the first time in her career, Crawford found her audience. And she fell in love. She was more loyal to her fans than to anyone. They, in turn, were loyal to her. They still are.

She was the most savvy of actresses; able to sense the winds of cultural change, then quickly tweak and update her image. When the Great Depression hit, Crawford's market instinct took over. Knowing she could not play the flapper forever, she fought for meatier roles. She read scripts and developed a good insight as to what the ordinary person was thinking. And taking cues from silent stars like Gloria Swanson and Lon Chaney, she combined her intense acting talent with the movie star charisma the studio wanted. By the early Thirties, the Joan Crawford we all know was born: the ambitious, hard working, sexy, fiercely independent (and furious!) woman.

Through films like Paid (1930), Letty Lynton and Rain (both 1932), she represented the Raging Woman of the Twentieth Century. The same woman, who ten years earlier, could not even vote. She had a direct impact on questioning the role of women in American culture. Her films are a precursor to the feminist movement of the 1960's. You don't own me! Nobody does!, she declares in Possessed (1931) as she leaves her sorry existence for a more fulfilling life in the big city. "My life belongs to me!!" That became the anthem of Crawford's life, her audience, and the accepted stance for all freethinking people. Watch this film today. Crawford's radiance has not dimmed. It has only grown stronger.

In Sadie McKee (1934), Crawford's character questions her situation at the height of the Depression. An unsympathetic person tells her to stop complaining. "What happened to you has happened to millions of other people!"..."Has it?!", she says, "I wouldn't know about that. I only know it's happened to ME." That statement strikes a cord with the audience. We don't care about the rhetoric of the politicians (prosperity is just around the corner). We can't relate to millions of people. But we can understand one person's struggle. And Crawford represents that.

By reinventing her screen image every decade, Crawford kept her audience guessing. In the Twenties, she was a flapper (Four Walls--1928). During the Thirties, she portrayed working class women (Rain, Mannequin-1938). She proved to the world she was a great actress by attacking more challenging roles in the Forties (A Woman's Face--1941, winning an Oscar for 1945's Mildred Pierce, Possessed--1947, another Oscar nomination). As moviegoers turned to sex goddesses and waifs like Marilyn Monroe and Audrey Hepburn in the Fifties, Crawford grew old with her audience.

At a time when most films about women dealt with femininity and charm (i.e., being and becoming a good wife and mother), Joan wasn't afraid to play headstrong aging women (Johnny Guitar--1954, Queen Bee--1955). And in the Sixties, she used her star persona against herself and gave some wildly melodramatic performances in horror films, thus tapping into the youth market (Whatever Happened to Baby Jane?--1962, Strait Jacket--1964).

In Crawford's real life, maintaining a movie career that was (and still is) hostile to a woman over forty is nothing short of a miracle. With her fourth and final marriage to Pepsi-Cola president Alfred Steele, Crawford became a successful businesswoman with the company in the 1950's. After Steele's death, she worked for Pepsi and acted in films and television until her death in 1977. In her best films (Grand Hotel, Humoresque--1946, Sudden Fear--1952), she is one of the greatest actresses of Hollywood's Golden Era. Even in her worst films, Crawford is always intriguing; never boring. Having viewed most of Crawford's eighty-one films, I have yet to see one of her character's whine about her lot in life.

I see a woman who faces reality and does not rely on some guy to bail her out. In the film noir classic, Sudden Fear, she plays a famous playwright who marries a younger man (Jack Palance). Unlike many films of the 1950's, her happiness does not depend on the security of a man (after all, she's the one who is rich). And Crawford's character is obviously passed child bearing years; hence, she does not seek happiness with a man through children. It is all too clear she marries this younger man for sexual fulfillment. After the film's whirlwind romantic first half, Crawford learns through a faulty recording playback that her hubby and his girlfriend are going to kill her for her money. Should Joan call the police? Hell, no! They would never believe a hysterical woman anyway.

Using her skills as a writer, she cleverly concocts a plan to murder her husband before he kills her--and pin it on the girlfriend! Rent this underrated thriller. It is suffice to ask, who needs a cop when Joan's around? Give her a mink and a gun--she is the woman for the job.

Joan Crawford will live forever as one of the icons of American Cinema. With that perfectly chiseled, authoritarian-defying face, she should be the monument that greets the immigrants at Ellis Island. All that wonderful anger and fury against a world of force and injustice. She stands alone. Yet we can relate to her individuality because she lived life on her own terms. In the tradition of all great artists and feminists and visionaries, Joan Crawford is an example for autonomous citizens everywhere. She is the ultimate American movie star. In short, the lady had guts!

I have mentioned previously that finding people in today's world who've had a personal one on one relationship with Joan is difficult. I was lucky enough to get a surprise e-mail from John Cohan, Psychic to the Stars, and long time friend of Joan. He'd heard about this book and he wanted to give me an insight into *his* relationship with Joan Crawford, movie star and friend.

Over the years, many celebrities have called on me, John Cohan, to give them a reading, an insight into their future. Whether it be their career or personal life, I have made a name for myself as "the celebrity Psychic." My Psychic columns have been in major newspapers and magazines; my full-page column ran in Soap Opera Weekly, once a week for a year. I've also been a part of Cindy Adams New York Post column for sixteen years, running with my yearly predictions and exclusives. I was also the resident Psychic on Joe Franklin's television show, the show is long gone but Joe and I remain close friends to this day.

I first came to meet Joan after she personally asked to see me through my friend, actress, Inger Stevens. That was my original, first meeting with Joan Crawford, the legend, on a one to one basis. I would visit her home, we would walk in the park, and many times, we'd have dinner at Sardi's, our favorite restaurant at the time. Joan would always order their fish and pasta dishes. She loved it when I made her my Eggplant Parmigiana, until I introduced her to that dish, she said she'd usually steer clear of eggplant. But she adored my recipe. To this day, I still make that dish and I can hear Joan saying how much she loved it.

Joan and I would talk about a variety of things; she needed my help with the many complex issues in her life. In person, Joan was a small woman, feminine, gracious, charming, a far cry from the larger than life screen persona that many of her fans saw in her movies. I know factually, from Joan, the children were always a handful. Joan was not a Mommie Dearest, but she did let Christina have it when she needed it, and she needed it, let me tell you! - That child was capable of causing someone to have a nervous breakdown, that's how uncontrollable she was.

As for Joan's love life, the common misconception is that Joan's great love that got away was the king of Hollywood, Clark Gable. She liked Clark Gable, she liked him a lot but as a lover in real life he wasn't a king like he portrayed on screen, far from it in the lover department...

As loved as she was by her fans, Joan was a very lonely woman. She often talked about how she regretted not marrying Yul Brynner when he proposed to her. She said he was a darling man to her and they maintained an on and off romance throughout the years. Yul confirmed this to me when I spoke to him too. He said that Joan offered him a real sweetness and tenderness that he never encountered before. He had met many actresses who faked those qualities, but didn't truly possess it. Joan really had it but kept it well hidden. She reserved it for the people she trusted and truly loved.

Yes, Yul Brynner was known as a womanizer, but according to Joan, his love for her was different, he showed none of that "love 'em and leave 'em" attitude with her, ever. As much as Joan claimed that Pepsi boss Alfred Steele was the love of her life, he wasn't. She said he was a kind, nice man to her, but he pampered her like a china doll, not like a woman. He adored Joan but he couldn't give her the "I feel the earth move" closeness that a man gives a woman. He thought his china doll would break if he didn't protect her from simple, earthy things. Joan told me that on screen she liked being the Queen Bee, but in love, in reality, in life, she wanted nothing else but to be a woman. Alfred could never resign himself to that kind of reality.

As to "that feud" with Bette Davis. Yes, it was real, very real. Joan hated Bette with a passion because she had a way of sticking it to you out of the blue, unplanned, but making it cut very deep! She told me that she really was very ill when she started work on "Hush...Hush, Sweet Charlotte" with Bette Davis. Joan said to me, "Johnny, if I really wasn't deadly sick, do you think in this lifetime I would miss the opportunity to slap the hell out of Bette Davis?!"

In 'Hush, Hush,' Joan's character did have the opportunity to slap Bette. In "Baby Jane" Bette beats the hell out of Joan, so 'Hush, Hush,' was payback time for Joan. Sadly, she had to leave the production and Olivia DeHavilland, who was Bette's real life friend, replaced her. Joan always regretted not being able to do, 'Hush...Hush, Sweet Charlotte.'

From all the conversations we had over the years, I feel that Joan ended her own life, though she did indeed have cancer. She said I was an angel in helping her through her problems and just being there to listen to her, but despite her success, there were deep emotional scars from her young life that were always there to haunt her. Shortly before she died she talked to me about the treatment she received at a party that she had gone to, she wore a wig because her own hair was unmanageable. According to Joan, the people at the party were terribly mean to her, especially reporter, Rex Reed, who was vicious. Joan said he gave the definition, "old queen with claws out" a new meaning!

I have a beautiful watch that Joan gave me; she said it had saved her life in two car accidents. It was her lucky charm and she wanted me to have it. Unfortunately, I don't have a photo of me with Joan; we talked so much, we just never got around to taking photos, I guess. In closing, Joan Crawford was a real lady, well poised, elegant, all qualities that hardly exist in today's world. She was a true friend, a wonderful woman, a legend.

Many of the candid snapshots within this book, a majority of which, until now, have remained unpublished, were generously donated from the extensive, Sobek Archive Collection. Sean Sobek, a lifelong Hollywood Historian, shares his view on why Joan Crawford became a movie industry icon, and why, after all these years, she continues to be worshipped by a legion of fans, a majority of which were born *after* her death. This is his theory -

Hollywood is more than just a city in California; it is a state of mind and the source of most of America's folklore. It has a history that is unique to any time or country and because of its universal marvel is as important as any other legendary city of any time and it should not be dismissed as just entertainment. Although its history is a little too recent for many people today to take seriously, our film library contains the most tangible record of American life, culture and values.

The most magical era of Hollywood was the early years. Today there are more celebrities than stars, but in its heyday its offspring were extraordinary figures projected all over the world. One of its more famous progeny was Joan Crawford. She is a representative of an age whose glamour is romanticized today. It was a time of formalities, etiquette, penmanship and a time when hard work was a source of pride. A time when dressing up was more of a privilege than a nuisance and if you were lucky enough to have fans, you were more grateful than guarded. Joan embodied that fabled era known as the Golden Age of Hollywood and together they were born, raised, grew up and older, became passé, died and became fodder for legend.

Joan's early years are the subject of much conjecture since it was retrospectively pieced together through recollections of various people. Nonetheless the common denominator was that Joan did not have a happy childhood and she put it behind her swiftly and permanently when she was yanked from middle school. (Forged documents allowed her to attend college, but it was a short-lived stint). As soon as it was feasible she used *whatever means necessary to get out of Small Town, USA. Equipped with only an incredible work ethic and the steely determination never to return to the poverty that plagued her youth, Joan would become a success.*

After all, acting was never her aspiration and it may not have even been her God-given talent, yet she had one of the longest and most varied careers in Hollywood with successes in almost every genre. From silent films to musicals, comedies to horror films and a hefty dose of melodramas thrown in for good measure, Joan played everything from ingénues to spinsters accordingly receiving several Academy Award nominations and a win in 1946. Joan was always extremely grateful -- not only to the film industry for giving her the opportunity to become a success, but also to her fans. It is fair to say that Joan's enthusiasm for her fans was matched by their enthusiasm for her. When the films became less frequent, she stepped into the executive world of Pepsi-Cola culminating in her receipt of one of the first national awards of The Ten Outstanding Women in Business before her retirement as she closed in on age seventy.

She was also a mother to four children after pioneering the way for single parents to adopt. When Joan's eldest child neared the age of forty, it dawned on her that she had been abused at the hand of Joan. So a self-serving memoir was penned of her life entitled 'Mommie Dearest.' Over the years, 'Mommie Dearest' has become little more than a footnote in the legend of Joan Crawford. It is important to note that there's a difference between Joan Crawford – actress, and 'Mommie Dearest' -- camp icon, the latter being the joined forces of the Christina's perspective and Faye Dunaway's on-screen portrayal.

Although I believe that her daughter perceives these childhood memories as truth, it's never prudent to take one person's perspective of a conflict as gospel – particularly when the other side is silent. Many children of that era had similar upbringings but were never considered "abused," but because of Joan's celebrity, she was held to a higher standard. And Joan's tough on-screen image made a spillover of character seem not only feasible but also probable thus making the book seem practical and Joan seem downright sinister.

To commemorate the 20th anniversary of the release of her book, 'Mommie Dearest,' the author now had new, worse revelations. But the shock waves were few; how many people now care to hear a sixty-five year old woman complaining about her dead mother? To bolster attention personal appearances were made. And into the word "camp" was breathed new life as the author handed out ornamented wire hangers to the interviewer and the participating manly Joan Crawford drag queen.

The hostility displayed by the author in recent interviews regarding her 20th anniversary edition is now revealing more about the author of the book than its subject. In a segment near the end of her book Christina intended to disgrace Joan, writing, "How could one woman carry so much hatred all those years – I thought it would have eaten her alive…" Today that seems eerily ironic.

Joan still remains a criterion for Hollywood glamour and new stars. There was something bewitching about her on-screen-- even though she didn't always make memorable films. Whether you liked her or not your eye was drawn to her no matter who she was paired with. And she's still celebrated without the benefit of having the landmark films of some of her contemporaries. She helped define fashion, career women and Hollywood's royalty, and that's how she'll be immortalized.

Aside from being a wife, mother, businesswoman and movie star, Joan was a whiz in the kitchen, she loved to cook and entertain friends. Her meatloaf recipe is one of her more famous cuisines. What better way to remember her than to pass around this delicious, yet easy recipe. Here it is, exactly as Joan used to make it. An all American recipe from an all American girl.

Joan Crawford's Meatloaf
2 pounds ground sirloin
1-pound ground veal
1 pound bulk sausage
3 raw eggs
1 large onion, finely chopped
2 green peppers, finely chopped
1 tablespoon seasoned salt
1 tablespoon Worcestershire sauce
1-teaspoon steak sauce
4 hard cooked eggs
2 tablespoon seasoned salt
2 tablespoon Worcestershire sauce
2-teaspoon steak sauce
1-cup water

Combine meats, unbeaten eggs, chopped onions and pepper, 1 tablespoon seasoned salt, 1 tablespoon Worcestershire sauce, and 1-teaspoon steak sauce. Mix thoroughly.

Shape mixture into oval loaf in shallow baking pan. Gently press hard cooked eggs into centre of loaf. Sprinkle with 2 tablespoons seasoned salt, 2 tablespoons Worcestershire sauce, and 2 teaspoons of steak sauce on top of loaf.

Pour 1 cup of water into pan. Do not pour over meatloaf once sauce has been put on. Bake in pre heated 350 degree F. oven for 30

215

minutes. Turn oven down to 300 degrees F. and bake for 30 minutes, then turn down to 250 degrees F. and bake for 45 minutes to 1 hour, basting frequently with pan juices.

Renowned photographer, John Engstead, spoke of his final photo session with Joan. He had taken portrait shots of her in 1945 and 1955, but it was this 1976 session that he remembered most. Sadly, it was her last.

"It was the late summer of 1976 and I had arrived at Joan's apartment at 12:30 for a one o'clock appointment. Not only was Joan ready but so was the apartment. She had covered all the carpets where we would work with heavy white canvas, and the chairs with plastic.

Joan answered the door (there was no maid), barefoot. Her hair had turned gray since I had seen her last, but her strong black eyebrows were a little at war with the new gray hair. The apartment was in lively colors of green, yellow and white. The place was immaculate -- not a thing, even, on the counters of the all-white kitchen. At 2:30 I left, since she had other appointments. This year I'll miss Joan's Christmas greeting -- always the first to arrive, and written by Joan herself."

This book is about Joan Crawford, the letter writer. However, as a young girl, Joan (then known as Billie Cassin), showed tremendous ability as a poet, and a professional writing career was not beyond her, had she chosen that artistic field. At the tender age of sixteen, the following poem, says a whole lot about a young woman, who ironically, would grow to crave love and acceptance, her entire life.

<u>Where Are You?</u> - By Billie Cassin

Where are you?
My heart cries out in agony
And in my extended hands I give my heart
With all its cries, its songs, its love
But, it's too late
You are not here to see its sorrow
Or hear its throbbing of your name
Perhaps it's better that way
You who love laughter
Did you ever know that I loved laughter too?
Oh, my beloved
Where are you?

Without a doubt, Joan Crawford was many things to many people. She's been quoted, written about, criticized and analyzed more than any other Hollywood star in the history of film. In fact, the American Film

Institute recently announced that she was # 10 on the list of the greatest screen legends of all time.

Still, I think legendary director George Cukor summed up Joan's life and legacy best of all. At the end of his emotional eulogy at her funeral, Cukor said, *"I thought Joan Crawford would never die. Come to think of it as long as celluloid holds together and the word 'Hollywood' means anything to anyone, she never will."*

Final Thoughts

"My fans are life and death to me, baby, they are the ones that really made me!"

- Joan Crawford.

I have often heard the phrase; *"A man can be a loyal and devoted friend to his buddies, but a terrible husband to his wife."* And, there's no reason why that situation can't apply in reverse, with a woman. Solely devoted to her friends, but not so good with her immediate family.

I have always tried to understand that split of absolute devotion on one side and that lack of devotion on the other. But, who of us is the perfect friend, husband, father, son or on the other hand, the perfect friend, wife, mother or daughter? - In all of those roles in life, it all comes down to *our perception* of perfection.

We all have many titles to bear in life, many expectations to live up to, but we "regular folk," lack the burden of one particularly crucial element that expects perfection in every one of those roles. The burden of fame. The microscopic existence of fame forces the public to expect that perfection from a movie star, and if they fail to live up to our perceived standards (not necessarily standards that we ourselves would live by) we eat them alive! - Why is that?

It's a given, movie stars, celebrities, are all a little bit prettier than us, they're all *a lot* richer than us, and they're photographed whenever they set foot into the outside world, no matter what the occasion. In comparison, us "regular folk" complain about our yearly birthday pose, and *that's* a photo we're prepared for. But in reality, movie stars exist to entertain us and "entertaining us" often goes beyond their performance on screen. In some cases, movie stars give far better performances in their personal lives, and the public are always going to be there to point the finger.

When will we realize that these people, these movie stars, are just us! - They're us with an upgrade. They're human, they make mistakes, it's as simple as that. So, why does pretty, rich, movie star, instantly equal perfection?   Not just in looks, but in behavior, in relationships, in everything!

This brings me back to Joan Crawford and *that* book. In the highly moralistic days when Joan Crawford made her career, the shocking tell all book, *Mommie Dearest*, was the first big Hollywood memoir written to tarnish the public perception of those golden days of old Hollywood, and all that it stood for.

Joan Crawford was a lot of things. She was the ultimate movie star, a smart businesswoman, a devoted friend, unlucky in love, and a mother. Yes, she was a mother. A mother who adopted four children that nobody else wanted, and she tried her damnedest to make them the best they could possibly be -- in *her* eyes. Her mothering was *her* perception of what was needed to mold her children into respectful adults. She did her best. Joan Crawford was not perfect, but I say it again -- who is?

It is without question, few actors had such a prolific career in the entertainment arena as Joan Crawford. Of course, I shouldn't neglect her many years with Pepsi either; she was a smart, tenacious businesswoman. Love her or hate her, she certainly deserves recognition for her longevity, her determination and her ability to reinvent herself enough to cater to an audience that spanned close to three generations of film goers.

Depending on your view on her actual year of birth, we're either in, or we're fast approaching the centennial year of Joan Crawford's entrance into the world. Whether it is a positive or negative viewpoint, most people of mixed ages, still know who Joan Crawford was and like many historical figures, she has become legendary.

In researching Joan's extensive film, television and radio career, I have answered many questions and even uncovered some interesting trivia relating to each individual project. However, I'm still yet to figure out the most important question of all. How did she possibly find the time to write *that* many letters?! The only explanation I can come up with is, she was Joan Crawford! Her fans were her life, her life was her work and her legacy of letters are a true testament to what it means to be a movie star.

****

So, go ahead, take a leaf out of Joan's book (literally), sit down and write an old fashioned letter to someone you care about. You'll be pleasantly surprised at the response...

219

Bibliography

Books

Brown, Peter Harry and Pamela Ann Brown. *The MGM Girls: Behind the Velvet Curtain*. New York: St Martin's Press, 1983.

Burrios, Richard. A Song in the Dark: The Birth of the Musical Film. ------ : Oxford University Press, 1997.

Castle, Charles. *Joan Crawford: The Raging Star*. ------: New English Library, 1977.

Considine, Shaun. *Bette and Joan:The Divine Feud*. New York: E.P Dutton, 1989.

Crawford, Christina. *Mommie Dearest*. New York: William Morrow, 1978.

Crawford, Joan with Jane Kesner Ardmore. *A Portrait of Joan*. New York: Doubleday, 1962.

Crawford, Joan. *My Way of Life*. New York: Simon & Schuster, 1971.

Engstead, John. *Star Shots*. New York: E.P. Dutton, 1980.

Guiles, Fred Lawrence. *Joan Crawford:The Last Word*. San Francisco, California: Birch Lane, 1995.

Hadleigh, Boze. *Bette Davis Speaks*. New Jersey: Barricade Books, 1996.

Higham, Charles. *The Celluloid Muse:Hollywood Directors Speak*. New York: Angus & Robertson, 1969.

Houseman, Victoria. *Made in Heaven:Unscrambling the Marriages and Children of Hollywood Stars*. Chicago, Illinois: Bonus Books, Inc., 1991.

Houston, David. *Jazz Baby*. New York: St Martin's Press, 1983.

Kidd, Charles. *Debrett Goes To Hollywood*. New York: St Martin's Press, 1986.

Kobal, John, ed. *Legends: Joan Crawford*. New York: Little Brown and Co., 1986.

Marx, Samuel. *Mayer & Thalberg: The Make Believe Saints*. New York: Random House, 1975.

McBride, Joseph. *Steven Spielberg:A Biography*. New York: Simon & Schuster, 1997.

Moore, Dick. *Twinkle, Twinkle, Little Star: And Don't Have Sex or Take the Car*. New York: Harper Collins, 1984.

Negulesco, Jean. *Things I Did..... and Things I Think I Did.* New York: Simon & Schuster, 1984.

Newquist, Roy. *Conversations with Joan Crawford*. New York: Citadel Press, 1980.

Olivier, Tarquin. *My Father:Laurence Olivier*. London: Headline Book Publishing, 1992.

Parish, James Robert with Don Stanke. *The Leading Ladies*. New York: Rainbow, 1979.

Peary, Danny. *Close Ups:The Movie Star Book*. Unknown: Workmen Publishing Group, 1983.

Quirk, Lawrence J. with William Schoell. *Joan Crawford:The Essential Biography*. Kentucky: University Press of Kentucky, 2002.

Riese, Randall: *All About Bette: Her Life From A-Z*. New York: McGraw-Hil, 1993..

Robertson, Patrick. *Film Facts*. New York: Billboard Books, 2001.

Schatz, Thomas. *The Genius of the System: Hollywood Filmmakin'*. New York: Pantheon Books, 1990.

Sherman, Vincent. *Studio Affairs: My Life As A Film Director*. Kentucky: University Press Of Kentucky, 1996.

Soares, Andre.*Beyond Paradise: The Life of Ramon Navarro*. New York: St Martin's Press, 2002.

Stine, Whitney. *I'd Love to Kiss You: Conversations With Bette Davis*. ------: Pocket Star, 1990.

Thomas, Bob. *Joan Crawford:A Biography*. New York: Simon and Schuster, 1978.

Walker, Alexander. *Joan Crawford: The Ultimate Star*. New York: Harper Collins, 1983.

Magazines and Newspapers

Crawford, Joan. "An Open Letter to Ed Sullivan From Joan Crawford." *Hollywood Magazine*, January, 1941, pp. -

Cross, Joan. "Name Her and Win $1,000." *Movie Weekly*, March 27, 1925, pp.. -

Flint, Peter B. "Joan Crawford Dies At Home." *The New York Daily News*, May 11, 1977, pp. -

Goulding, Morton J. "The Revolt of Joan Crawford's Daughter." *Redbook*, October, 1960, pp.-

Hollywood Magazine

Lansing State Journal. "Helen Hayes" Quote

Lilly, Doris. "Joan Crawford A Suicide: Doris Lilly Recalls the Stars Last 18 Months." *People Weekly*, May 30, 1977, pp. -

Marshman, Donald. "The Second Rise of Joan Crawford." *Life*, June 23, 1947, pp. -

Modern Screen Magazine - August, 1977

Motion Picture Herald

New York Herald Tribune - Richard Watts Jr.

Photoplay - (various)

Ribakove, Barbara. "At Last, I'm Finally Living the Life I Want." *Photoplay*, July, 1975, pp. -

Sachlar, Abram L. "A Host At Last." *Atlantic Monthly Press*, 1976 , pp. 161,162.

Sayer, Juanita. "I Chose A Wonderful Family." *Everywoman's*, 1952, pp. -

Silverman, Stephen M. "Daughter Dearest." *People Magazine*, May 6, 1998, pp. -

Walker, Helen Louise. "Joa Crawford: The Most Remarkable Girl In Hollywood." *Silver Screen*, January, 1934, pp. -

"Was She Devil or Doting Mom?: 'Dearest' Stirs A Row Among Joan Crawford's Adopted Kids." *People Magazine*, October 19, 1981, pp. -

Johnes, Carl. "Why Joan Crawford Won't Go Away: Part I and II." *Hollywood Then And Now*, August and September, 1992, pp. -

Internet Sources

Abe Books - www.abebooks.com

Brainy Quote - www.brainyquote.com

The Concluding Chapter of Crawford - www.theconcludingchapterofcrawford.cjb.net

Crime Magazine - www.crimemagazine.com

David Thompson - "Joan Dearest" - www.salon.com

Divas The Site - www.home2.planetinternet.be/verjans/divas.htm

EInsiders.com - Rusty White interview of Gary Gray.

E! News Online - www.eonline.com

Gallery of History - www.galleryofhistory.com

Goldberg Coins - www.goldbergcoins.com

Houle Rare Books and Autographs - http://abaa.org/usa/houle

Internet Movie Database - www.imdb.com

Jerry's Vintage Radio Logs - http://otrsite.com/radiolog

Joan Crawford Encyclopedia - www.joancrawfordbest.com

Joan Crawford Online - www.joancrawfordonline.com

Johnny Guitar Society - http://members.aol.com/michaemann/jgmain.html

Kenneth Rendell's K.W.R Gallery - www.kwrendell.com

The Knitting Circle - http://myweb.lsbu.ac.uk/~stafflag/williamhaines.html

Nitrate Online - www.nitrateonline.com

Odyssey Publications - www.autographs.com

Paul Festa - "Mommie Dearest In Drag" - www.salon.com

People Online - www.people.com

Proeme Autographs - www.vintagehollywood.net

R & R Enterprises - www.rrauction.com

Slipups - www.slipups.com

The Smoking Gun - www.thesmoking gun.com
Stinson Sports - www.stinsonsports.com
TV Guide Online - www.tvguide.com
The Unofficial Bette Davis Homepage -
http://my.execpc.com/~reva/html6b.htm
Venice Magazine - www.venicemag.com
World Entertainment News Network - www.wenn.com

Miscellaneous

Joan Crawford Live at Town Hall - Audio
Memo from the desk of David Selznick

Books based on or related to Joan Crawford films

Above Suspicion (novel, Helen MacInnes, 1941)
All the Brothers Were Valiant (novel, and basis for *Across to Singapore*;
Ben Ames Williams, 1919)
The Best of Everything (novel, Rona Jaffe, 1958)
Daisy Kenyon (novel, Elizabeth Janeway, 1945)
Dancing Lady (novel, James Warner Bellah)
The Gorgeous Hussy (novel, Samuel Hopkins Adams)
Humoresque and Other Stories (Fannie Hurst, 1919)
I Saw What You Did (novel, Ursula Curtiss)
Johnny Guitar (novel, Roy Chanslor, 1953)
Letty Lynton (novel, Marie Belloc Lowndes)
Menschen Im Hotel (German novel, basis for *Grand Hotel*; Vicki Baum,
1929)
Mildred Pierce (novel, James M. Cain, 1941)
Mildred Pierce (screenplay and essays, Albert J. LaValley, ed., 1980)
Not Too Narrow, Not Too Deep (novel, basis for *Strange Cargo;* Richard
Sale, 1936)
Old Clothes (movie tie-in novelization, Willard Mack, 1925)
The Only Thing (novel, Elinor Glyn)
Our Dancing Daughters (movie tie-in novelization, Winifred Van Duzer,
1928)
The Queen Bee (novel, Edna Lee, 1949)
Rain and Other Stories (W. Somerset Maugham, 1921)
The Story of Esther Costello (novel, Nicholas Monsarrat)
Sudden Fear (novel, Edna Sherry, 1948)
What Ever Happened to Baby Jane? (novel, Henry Farrell, 1960)
The Women: Mujeres (Spanish novelization of *The Women*, 1939.)

Acknowledgments

Matt, for making me laugh, everyday!

My parents, for supporting me in everything I do, no matter how wacky it may be!

My stepsons Josh and Reeve

Jean, thank you for sheltering us from the storm. You know what that means...

Pearl, my other mother in law.

Bev, for being a friend first and a sister-in law second.

Malcolm Watt - Johnny Guitar Society

William Van Atta

Garrett Williams, for hunting down those elusive letters amidst his busy schedule

Tod Mueller

Pepsi Cola Co.

Phyllis Diller, Glenda Jackson and Betsy Palmer for their personal memories

Jim De Marco

Michael Botsko - For the generous contribution of his letter collection

Bsabas A. Bennett, for his continued dedication to the memory of Joan Crawford.

Karen Adler Abramson - Brandeis University

LaVina Pratt

Mark Toscani

Jonathon Denson

Neil Maciejewski

John Cohan

Sean Sobek, for your devotion to Joan Crawford and your generosity in sharing her private letters and beautful photographs. You are a true friend.

Theo Pouros, for access to your collection of Joan Crawford letters.

Thank you very much to the legion of fans who got behind this book with the enthusiasm that I'd only ever to come expect from you all.

And last but not least, I am forever indebted to Joan's daughter, Cathy Crawford Lalonde. Thank you, Cathy, for generously allowing me to publish your mother's thoughts and words, for all the world to see. Thank you also to Carla and Casey, Joan's grandchildren. You were both an integral part of allowing this book to exist. Honestly, the hardest part about writing this book was finding the right words to thank you for being so receptive to my idea. I have come to realize, no words can truly express my gratitude. I just know somehow, somewhere, your mother, your grandmother...our Joan, is smiling.

Printed in the United Kingdom
by Lightning Source UK Ltd.
115613UKS00001B/227